SUPERCAR COLORING BOOK

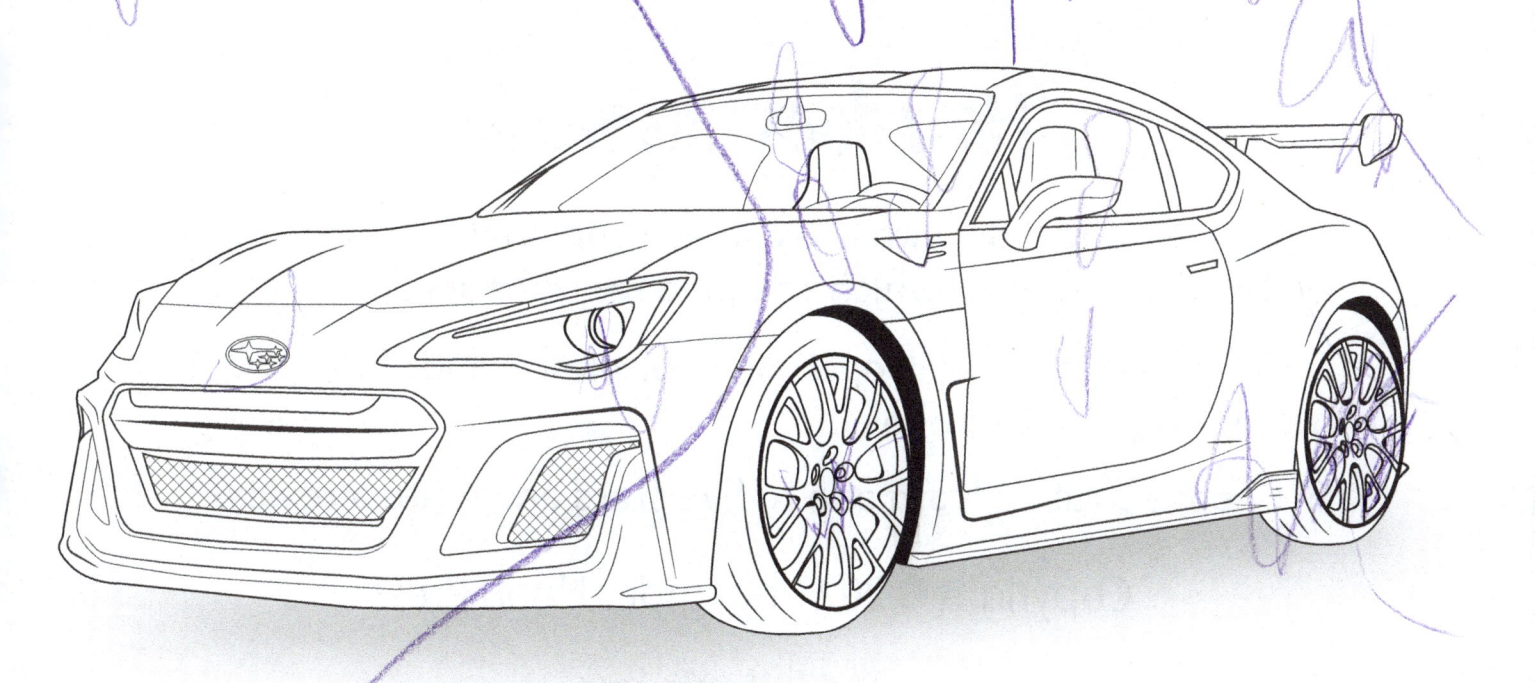

IF YOU WOULD LIKE TO SHOW YOUR SUPPORT, WE WOULD GREATLY APPRECIATE A RATING OR REVIEW ON AMAZON

Your ratings and reviews will help other colorists decide which books to purchase and encourage more people to begin the hobby of coloring.

Thank you for supporting Under Hood Press!

How does this work?

1. Scan this QR code with the camera app on your phone, based on the country from which you paid for the book.

2. The Amazon app will open on your phone and show you the rating page for this book.

3. Choose a rating from one to five stars and write a review.

Copyright © 2021 by Under Hood Press

All rights reserved.

BMW M4 COUPE

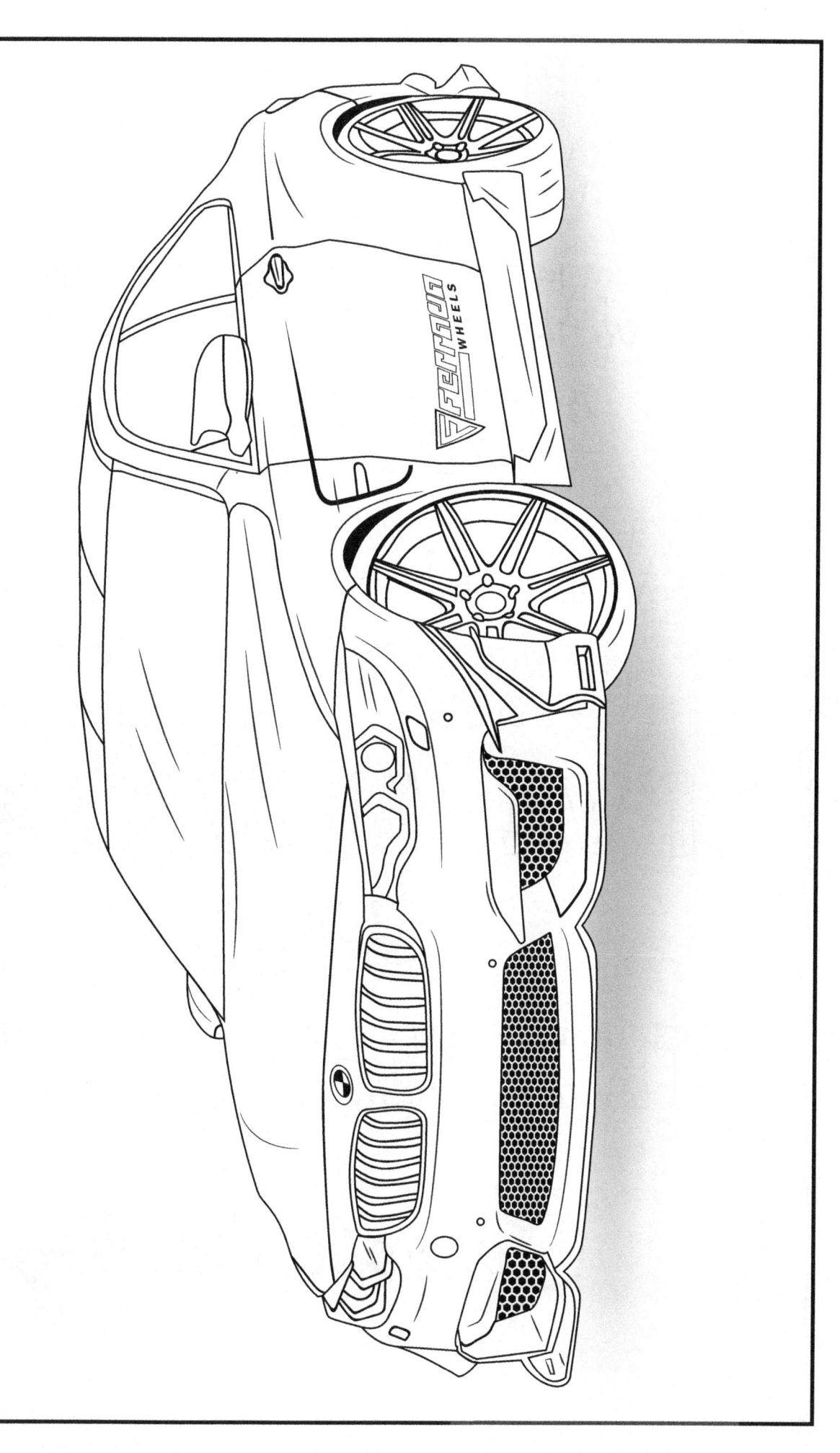

I'VE ALWAYS BEEN ASKED, "WHAT IS MY FAVORITE CAR?" AND I'VE ALWAYS SAID "THE NEXT ONE."

Carroll Shelby

ROLLS-ROYCE DAWN

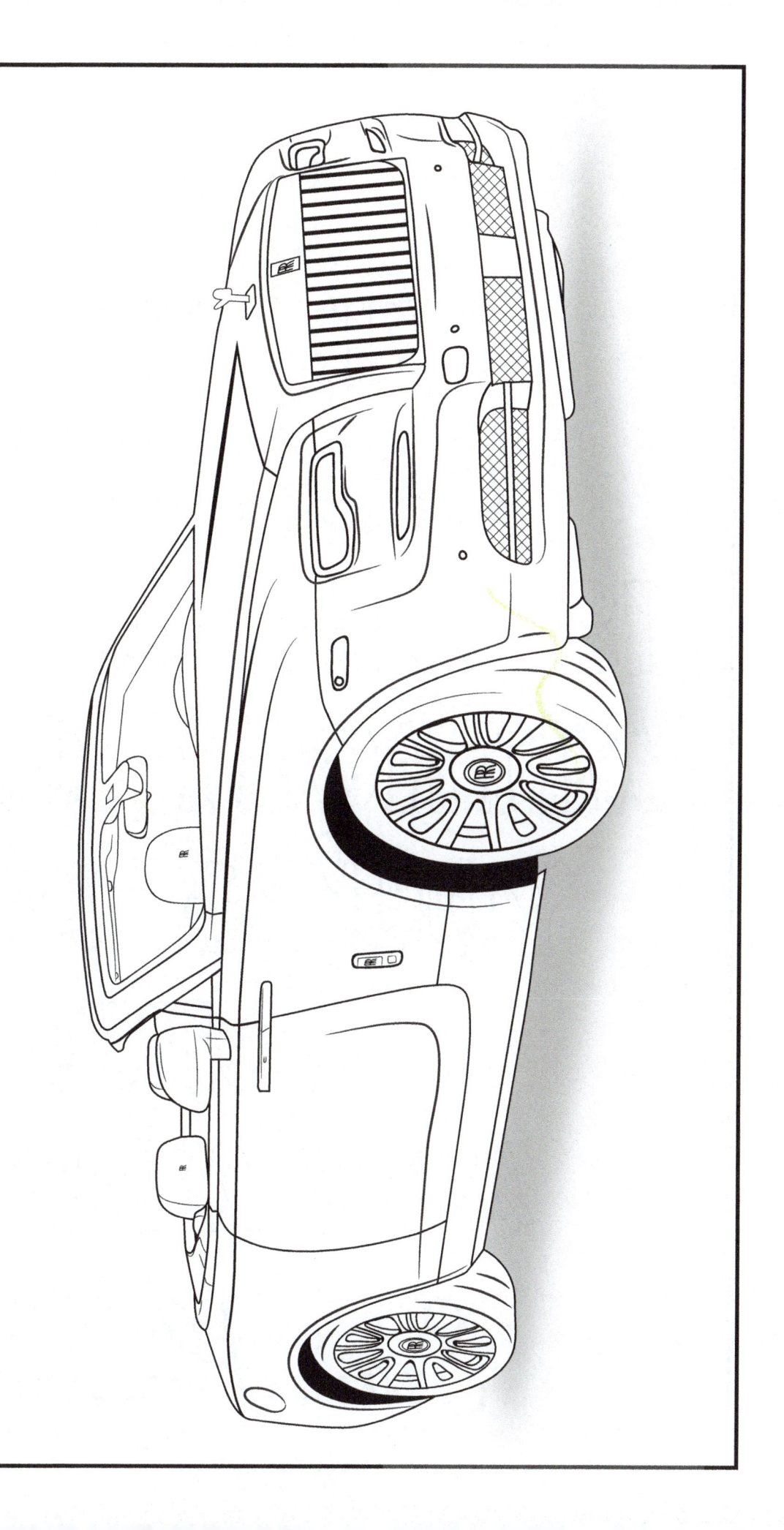

A DREAM WITHOUT AMBITION IS LIKE A CAR WITHOUT GAS... YOU'RE NOT GOING ANYWHERE.

Sean Hampton

LAMBORGHINI URUS

There's a lot of stress... but once you get in the car, all that goes out the window.

Dan Brown

AUDI TT

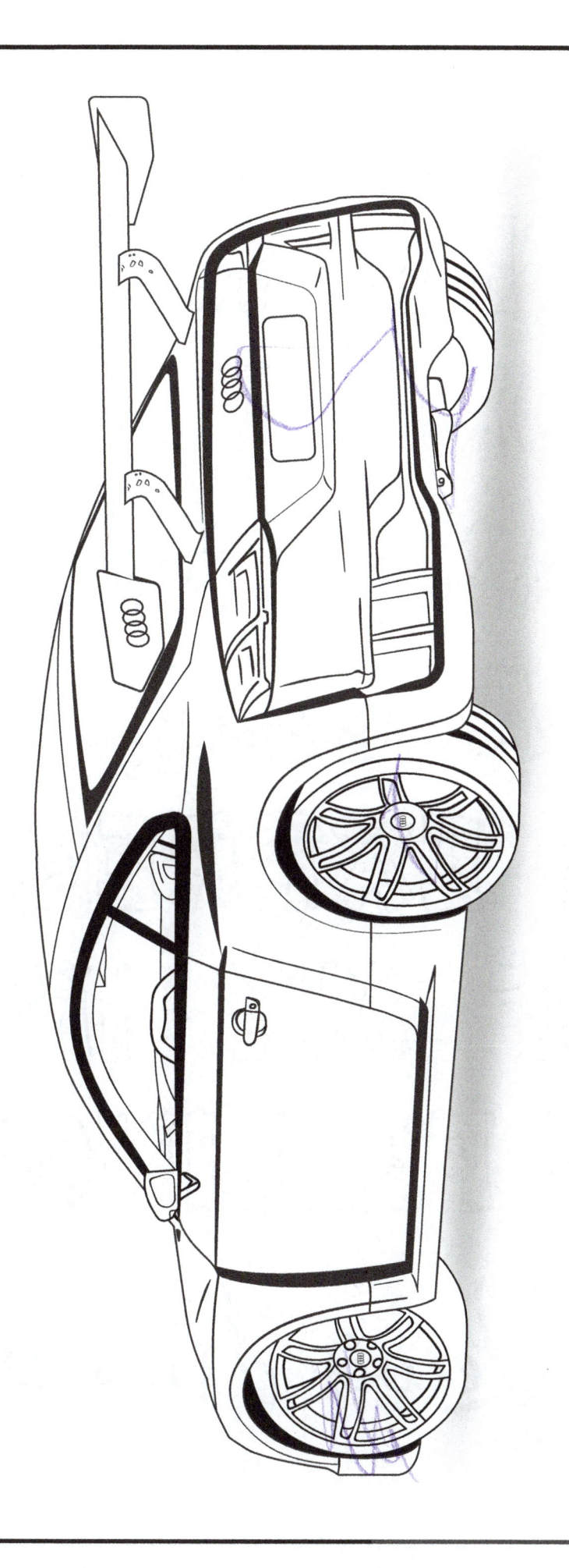

THE WAY I DRIVE, THE WAY I HANDLE A CAR, IS AN EXPRESSION OF MY INNER FEELINGS.

Lewis Hamilton

LAMBORGHINI
HURACAN

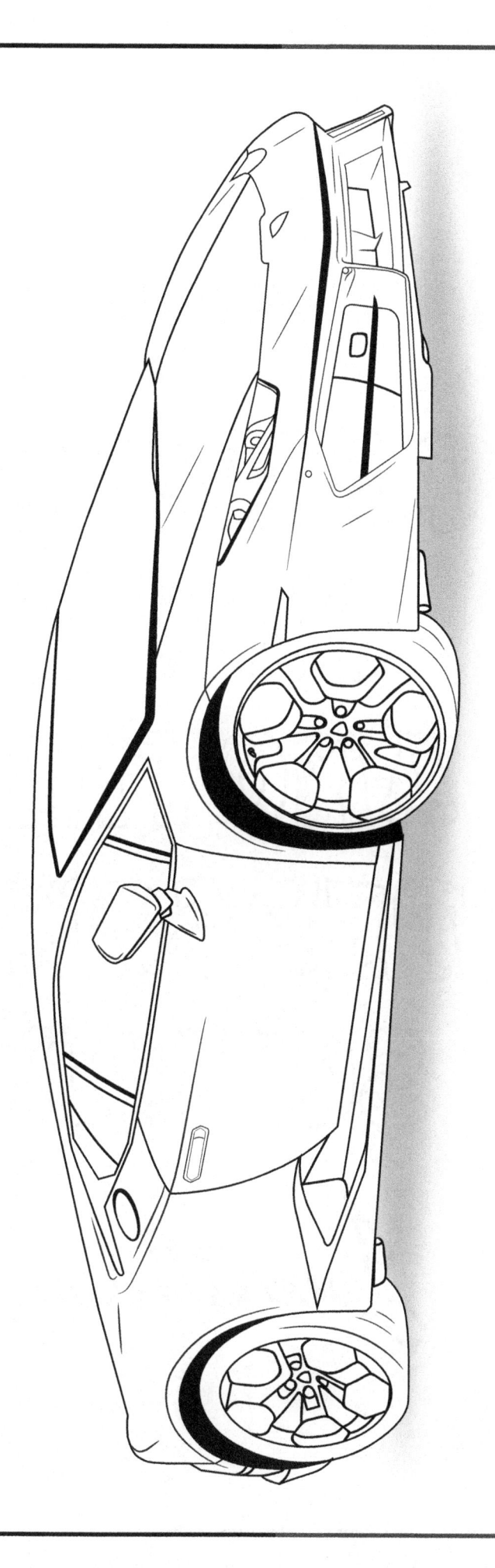

ONE PERSON'S CAR IS ANOTHER PERSON'S SCENERY.

Jonathan Ive

FERRARI F8 TRIBUTO

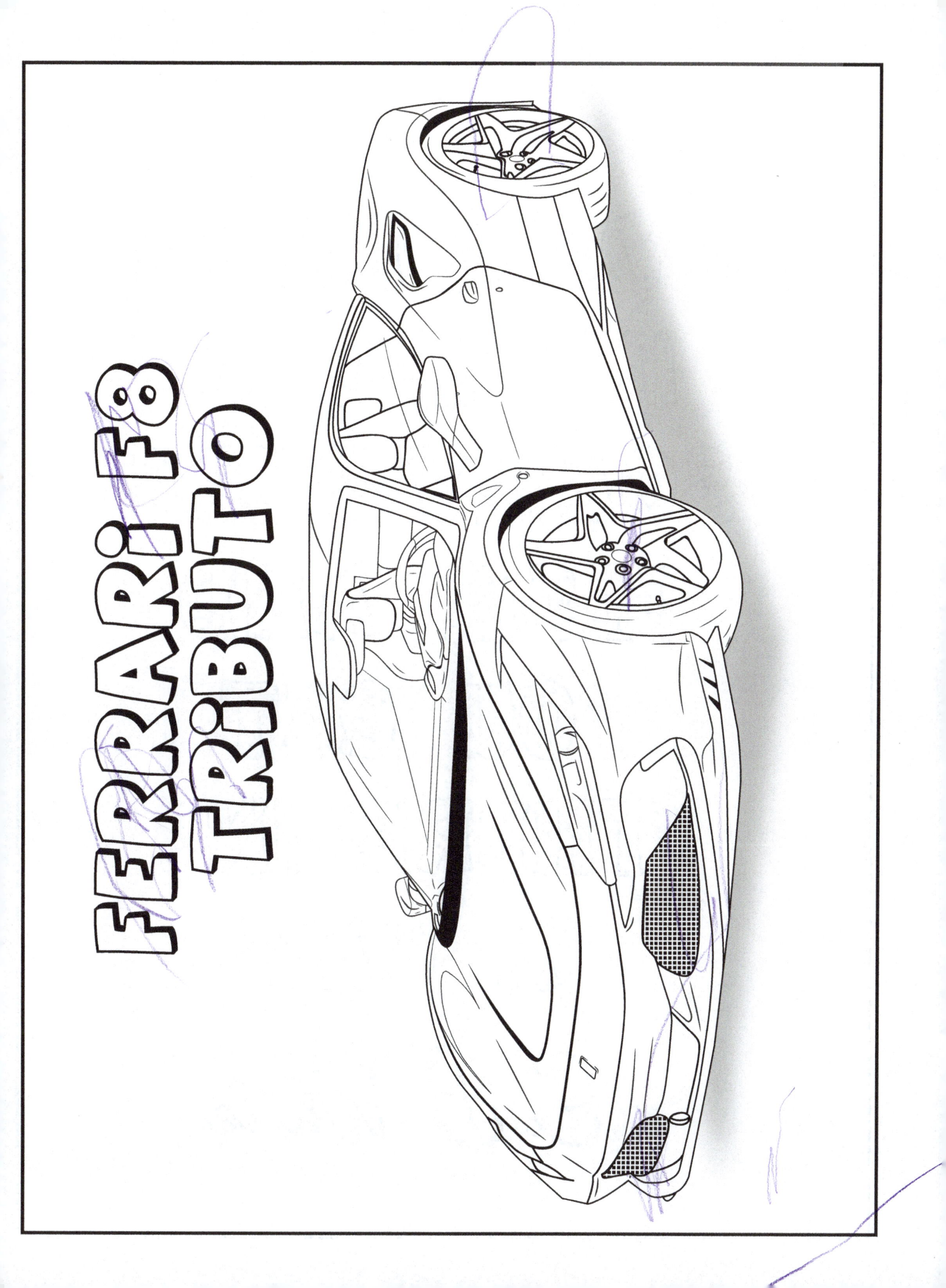

> Everything in life is somewhere else, and you get there in a car
>
> — E. B. White

FORD MUSTANG BOSS 302

THE FACT IS I DON'T DRIVE JUST TO GET FROM A TO B. I ENJOY FEELING THE CAR'S REACTIONS, BECOMING PART OF IT.

Enzo Ferrari

BMW 3 SERIES

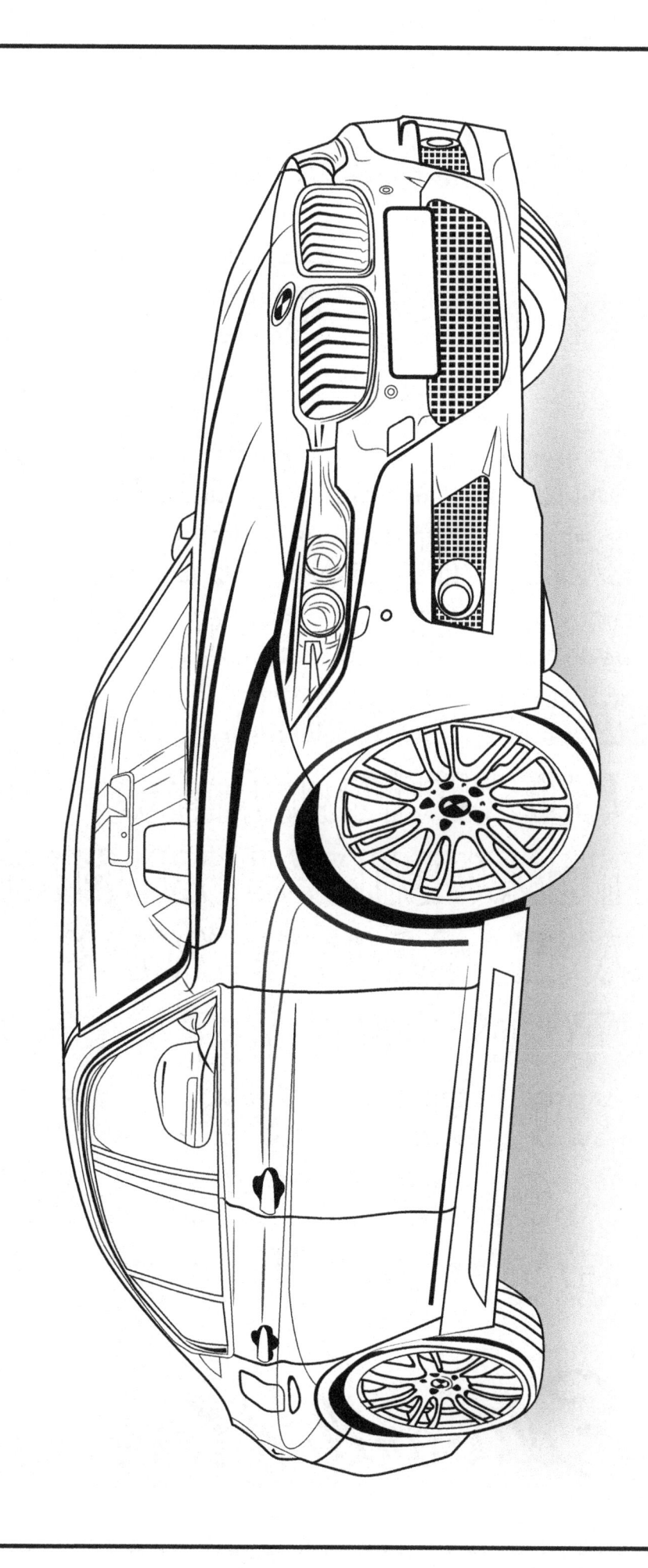

Automobiles have always been part of my life, and I'm sure they always will be. What is it about them that moves me? The sound of a great engine, the unity and uniqueness of an automobile's engineering and coachwork, the history of the company and the car, and, of course, the sheer beauty of the thing.

Edward Herrmann

CHEVROLET CAMARO ZL1

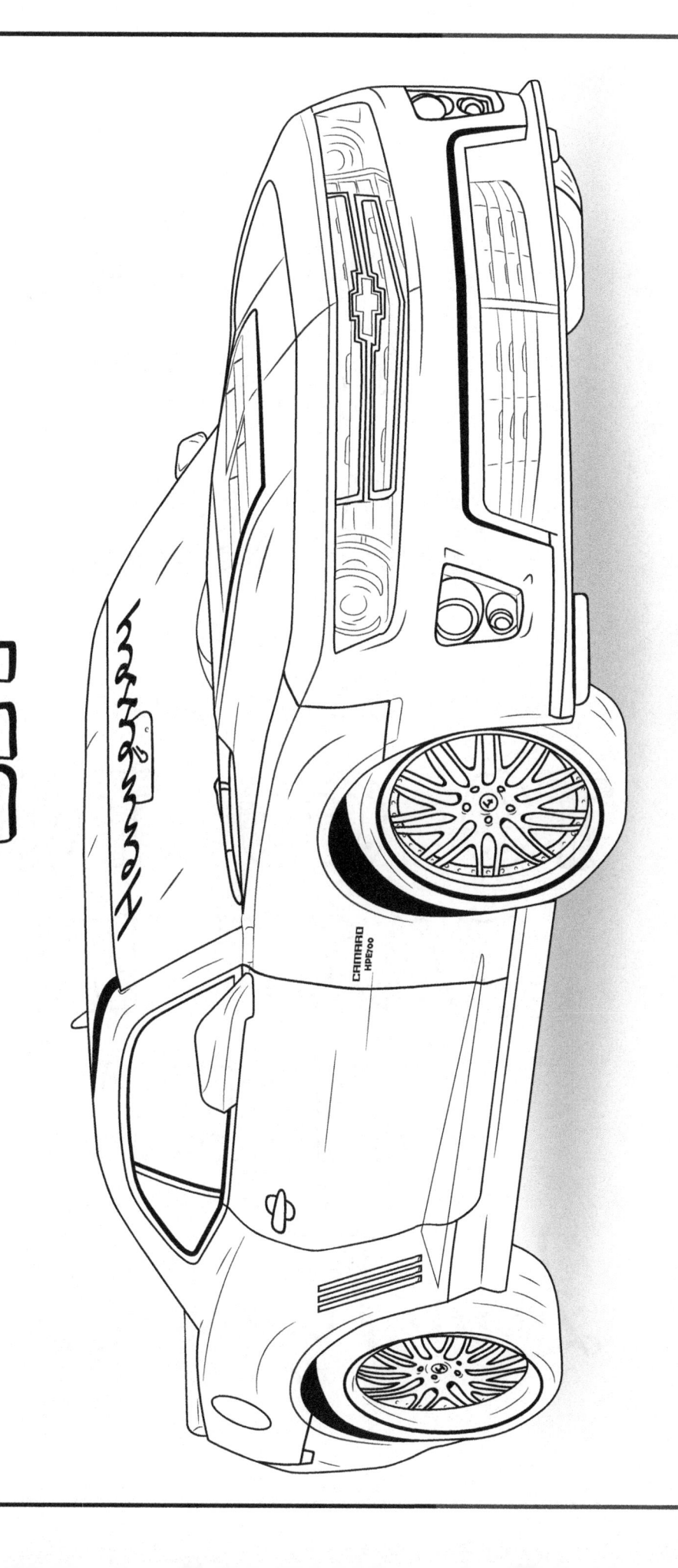

I LOVE FAST CARS... AND TO GO TOO FAST IN THEM.

Lara Flynn Boyle

FORD MUSHTANG

I'M A CRAZY CAR GUY. I'VE GOT AN AIRPLANE HANGAR FULL OF CARS.

Paul Walker

JEEP WRANGLER

Cars are the ultimate symbol of freedom, independence and individualism. They offer the freedom to 'go anywhere,' whenever it suits and with whom one chooses.

Sarah Redshaw

MASERATI GHIBLI

It's like driving your car. If you drive too fast on the highway, you will topple, so you better maintain your speed. Life is similar to that, and that's the way you have to control your head.

A. R. Rahman

AUDI R8

YOU'RE SAFER IN THE RACE CAR THAN YOU ARE IN CARS GOING TO AND FROM THE TRACK.

Mario Andretti

AUDI RS5 SPORTBACK

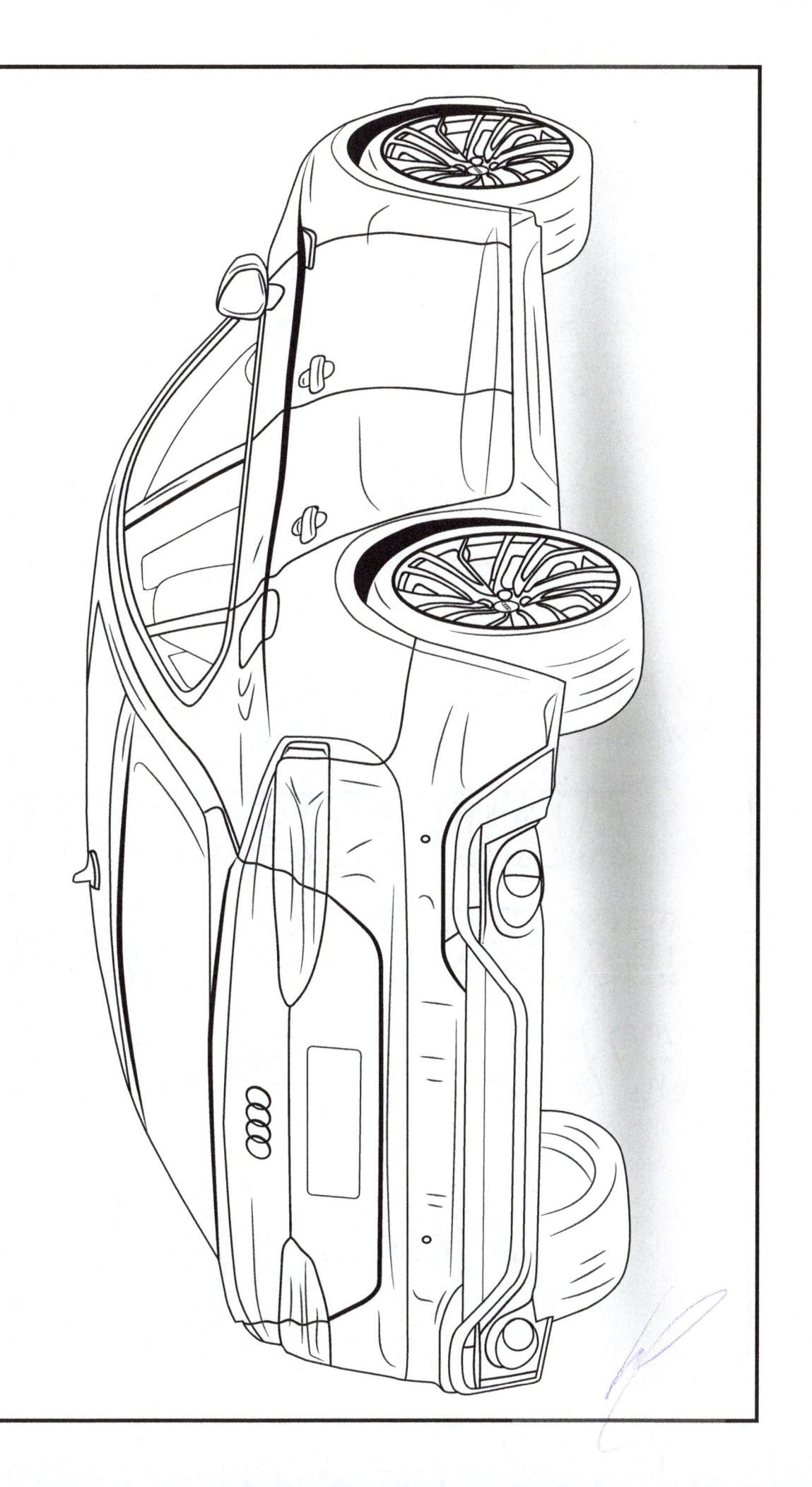

I KNOW A LOT ABOUT CARS, MAN. I CAN LOOK AT ANY CAR'S HEADLIGHTS AND TELL YOU EXACTLY WHICH WAY IT'S COMING.

Mitch Hedberg

FERRARI F12 BERLINETTA

See, when you drive home today, you've got a big windshield on the front of your car. And you've got a little bitty rearview mirror. And the reason the windshield is so large and the rearview mirror is so small is because what's happened in your past is not near as important as what's in your future. Joel Osteen Women are like cars: we all want a Ferrari, sometimes want a pickup truck, and end up with a station wagon.

Tim Allen

FORD SHELBY COBRA

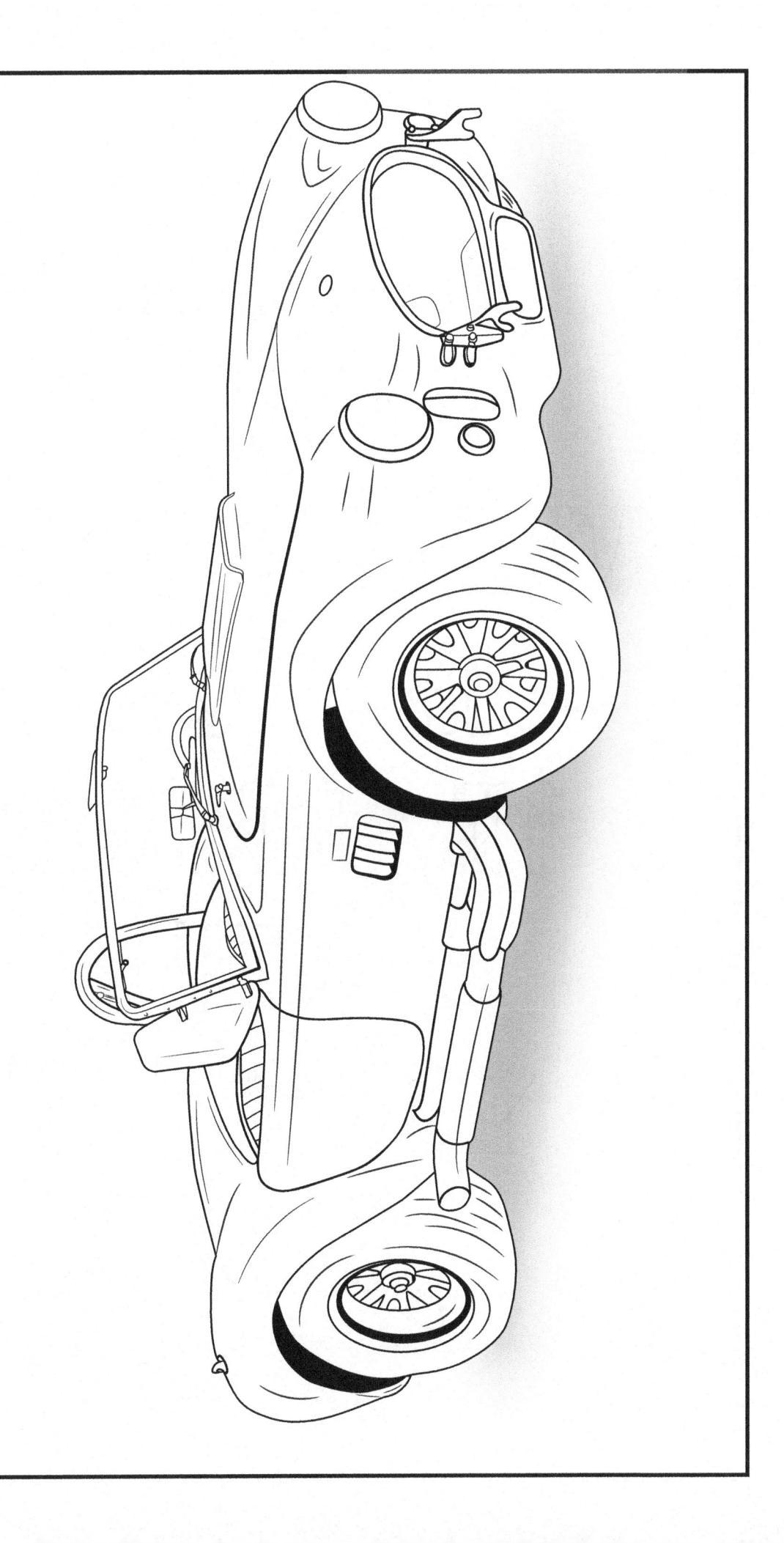

A CAR IS LIKE A MOTHER-IN-LAW – IF YOU LET IT, IT WILL RULE YOUR LIFE.

Jaime Lerner

HONDA NSX

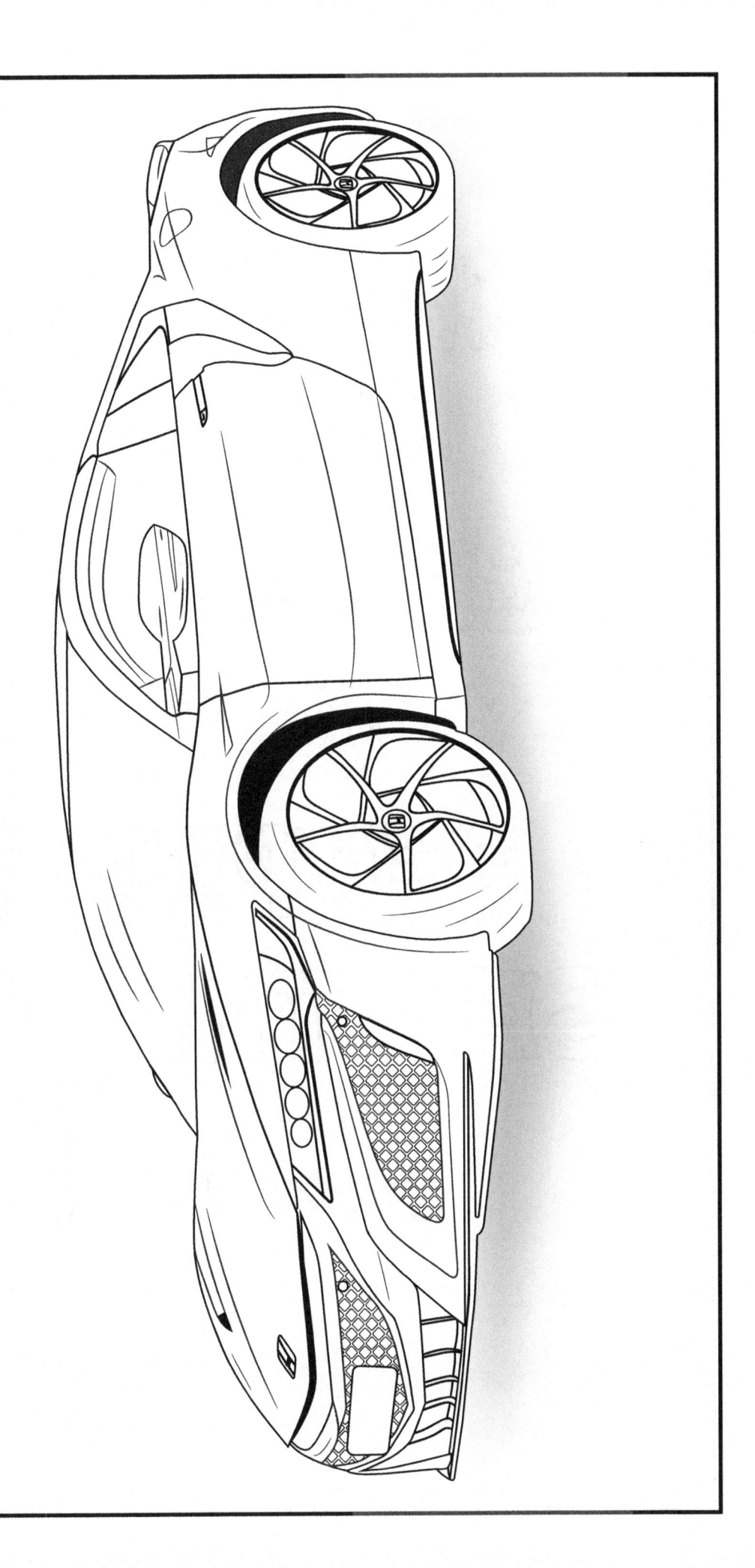

When you have a great car, you want people to see the car.

Andris Nelsons

MERCEDES-BENZ AMG GT COUPE

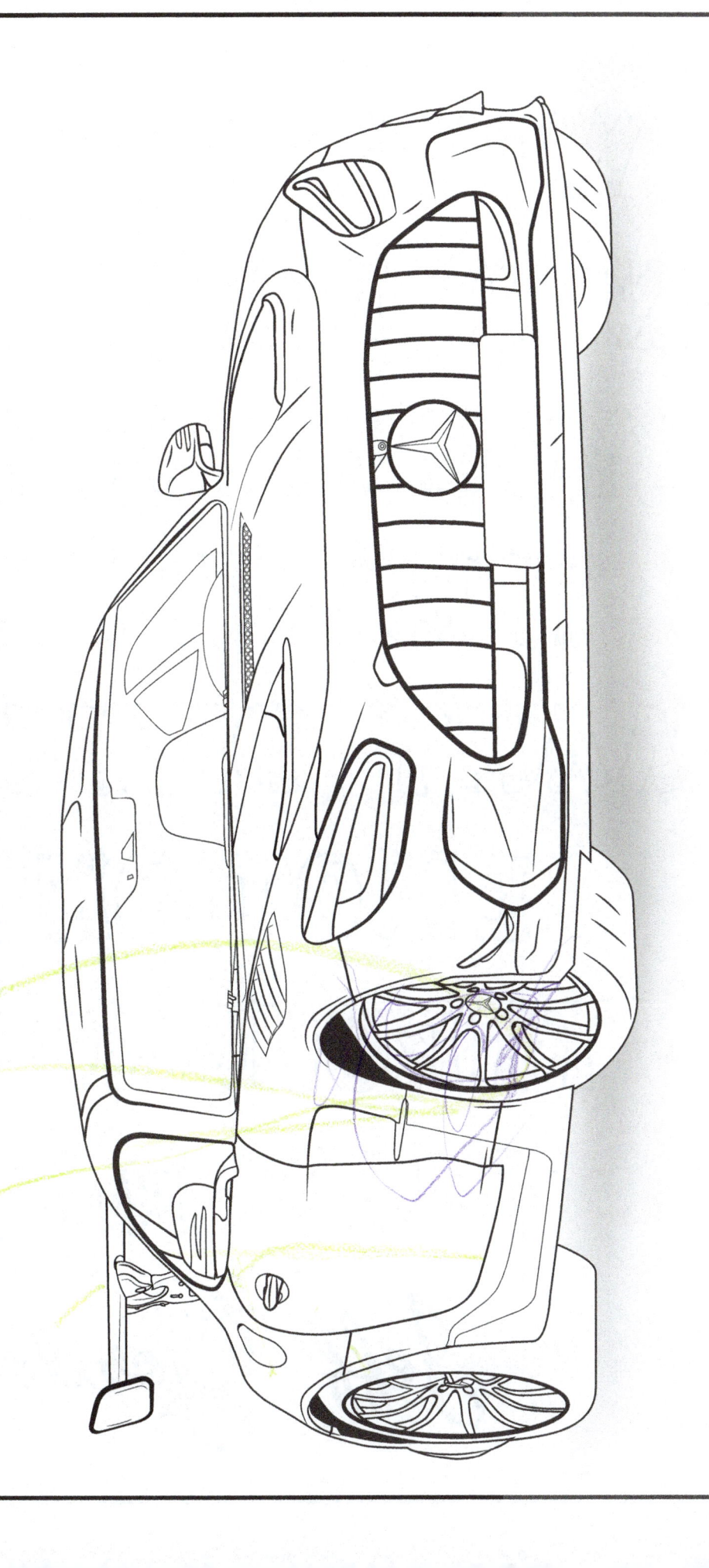

When you're in a race car, you're going through so many different emotions throughout that race.

Jeff Gordon

MERCEDES-BENZ G-CLASS

I love everything from old-school cars to whatever the latest muscle or luxury vehicles are.

Ludacris

PORSCHE 911 CARRERA

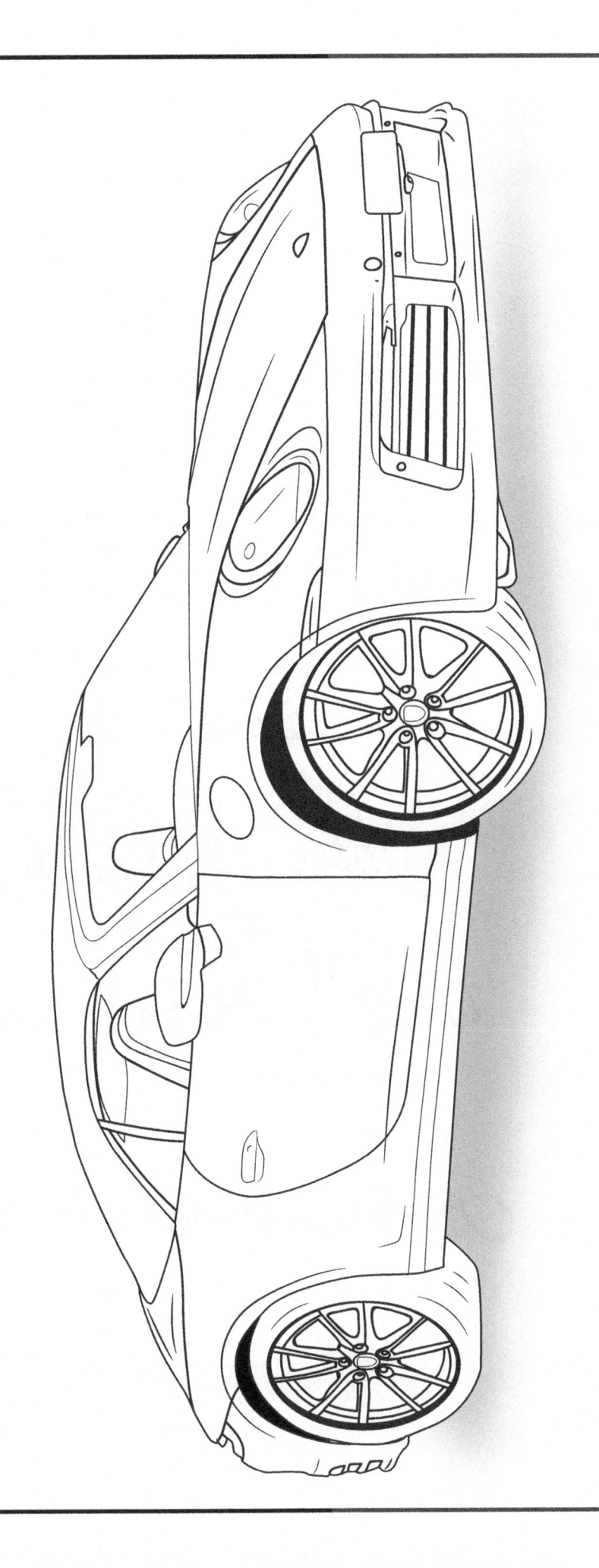

THE CARS
WE DRIVE
SAY
A LOT
ABOUT US.

Alexandra Paul

FERRARI 458 SPIDER

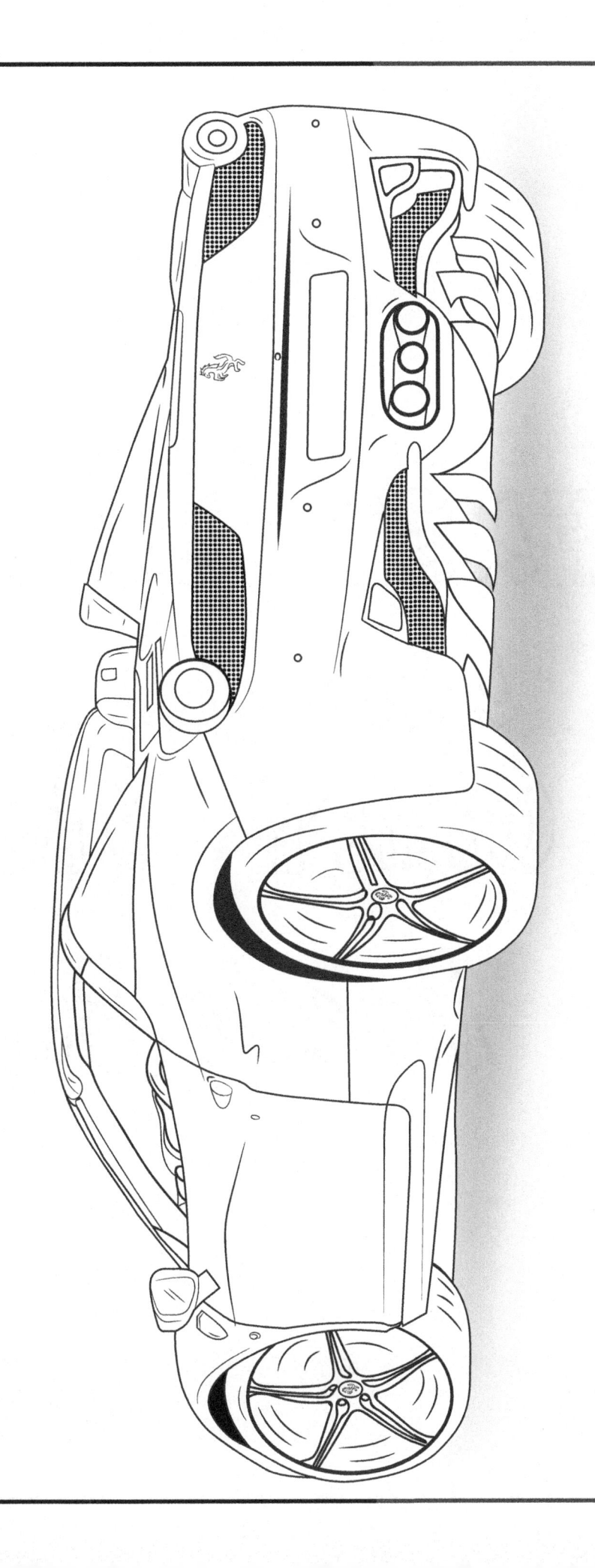

FAST CARS ARE MY ONLY VICE

Michael Bay

BMW Z4

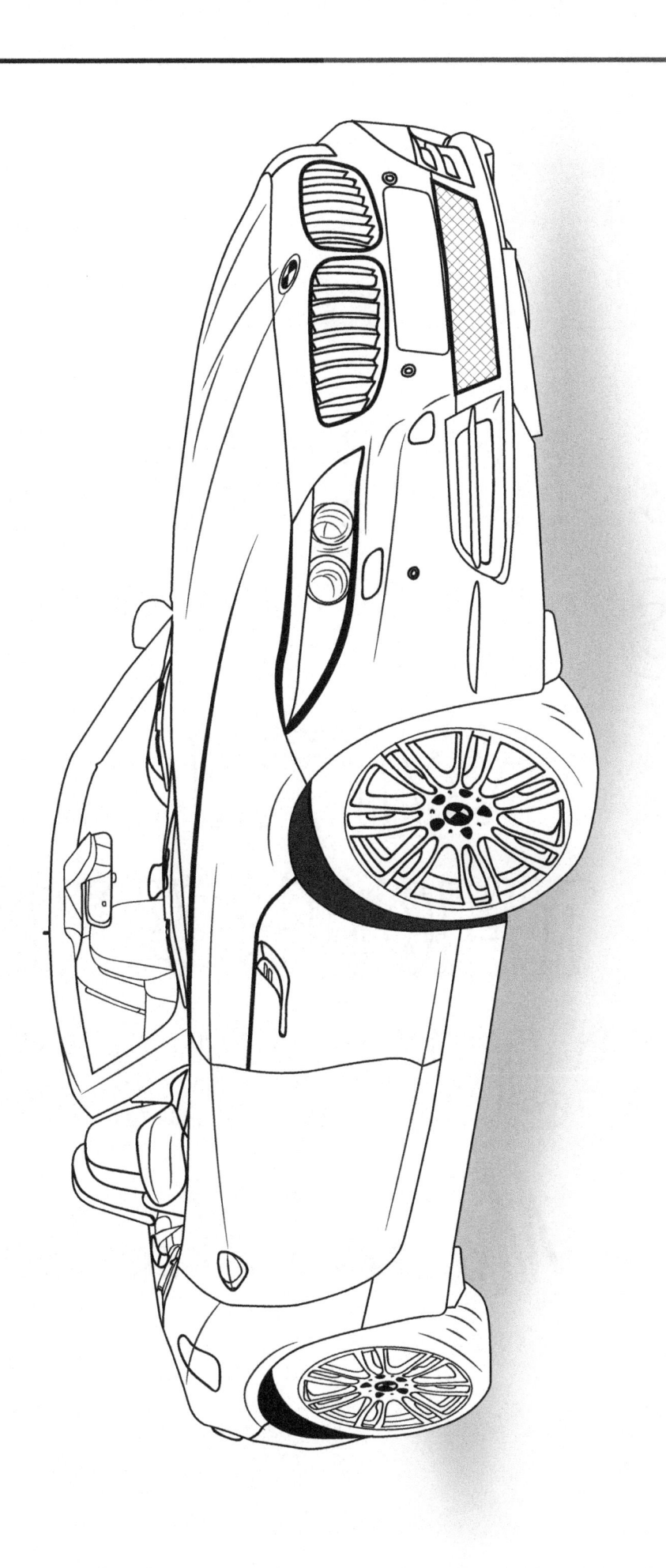

A RACING CAR IS AN ANIMAL WITH A THOUSAND ADJUSTMENTS.

Mario Andretti

LEXUS LC 500

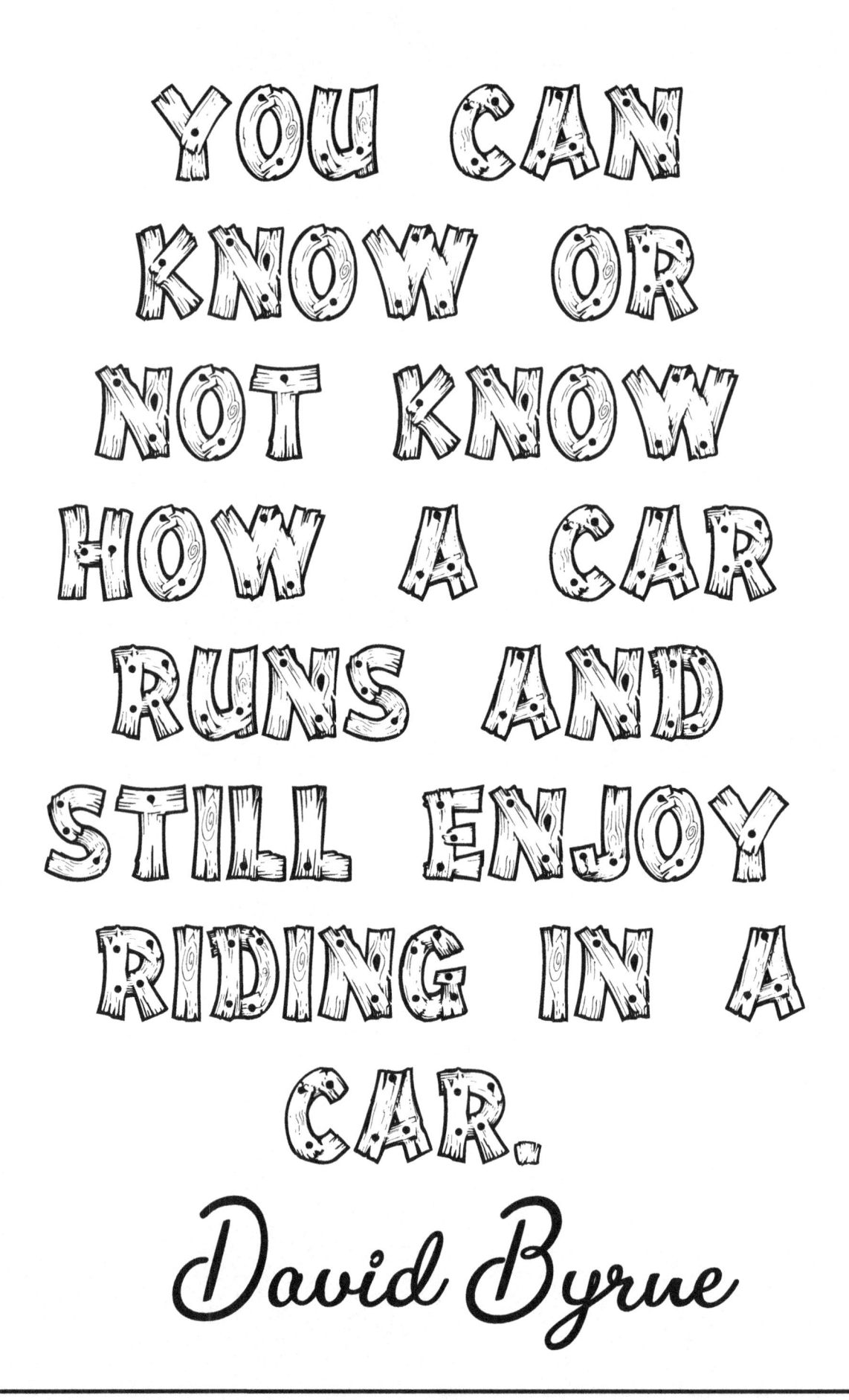

You can know or not know how a car runs and still enjoy riding in a car.

David Byrne

FORD MUSTANG

Generally, cars were not built to sit on dealer lots. It encourages the wrong kind of behavior in the whole system.

Rick Wagoner

AUDI A5 SPORTBACK

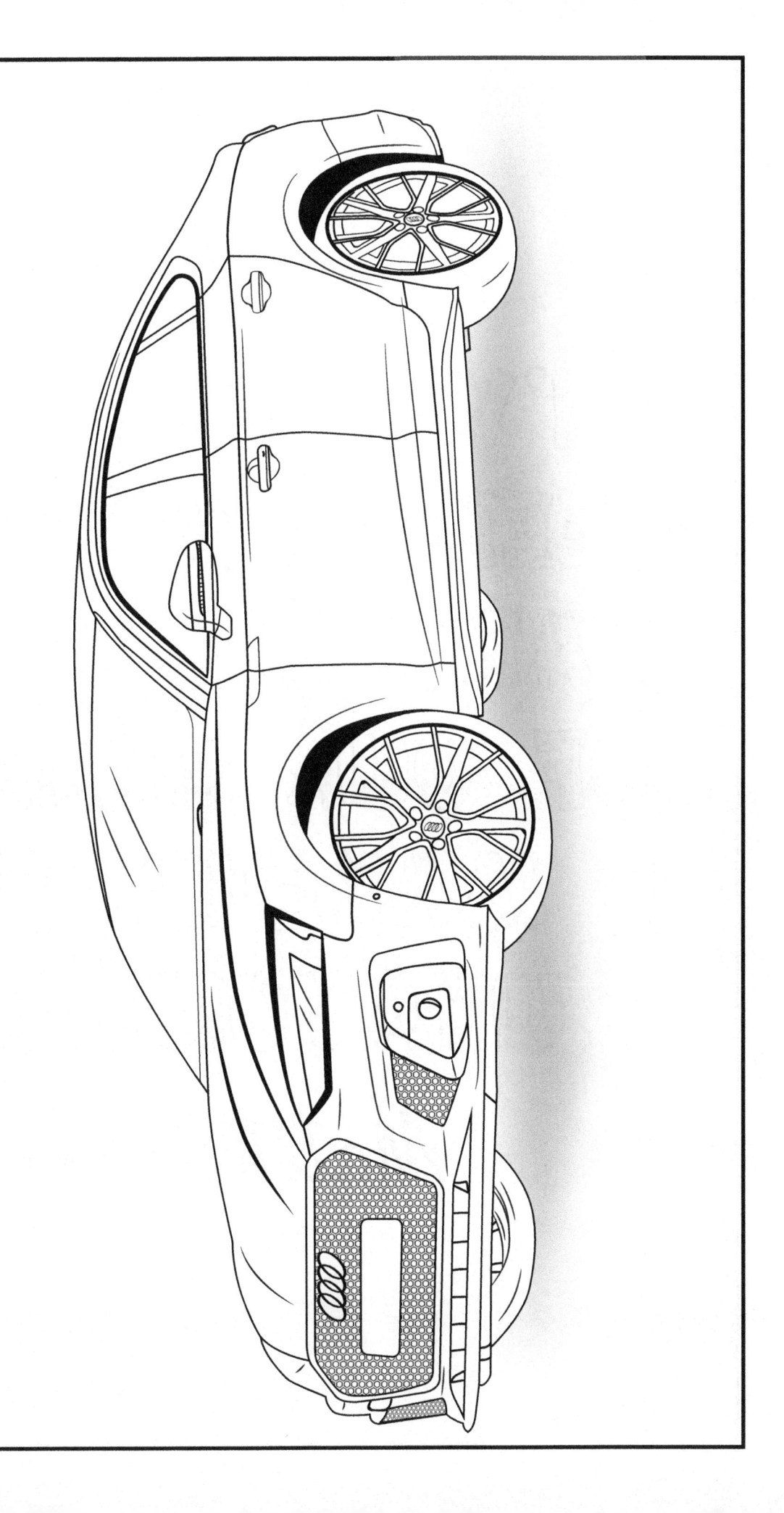

I'VE ALWAYS BEEN INTO CARS. CARS ARE PART OF OUR GENETIC MAKEUP. IT'S UNAVOIDABLE.

Matthew Fox

BMW 420i COUPE

I THOUGHT CARS WERE ESSENTIAL INGREDIENTS OF LIFE ITSELF.

Edward Herrmann

BMW M4 COUPE

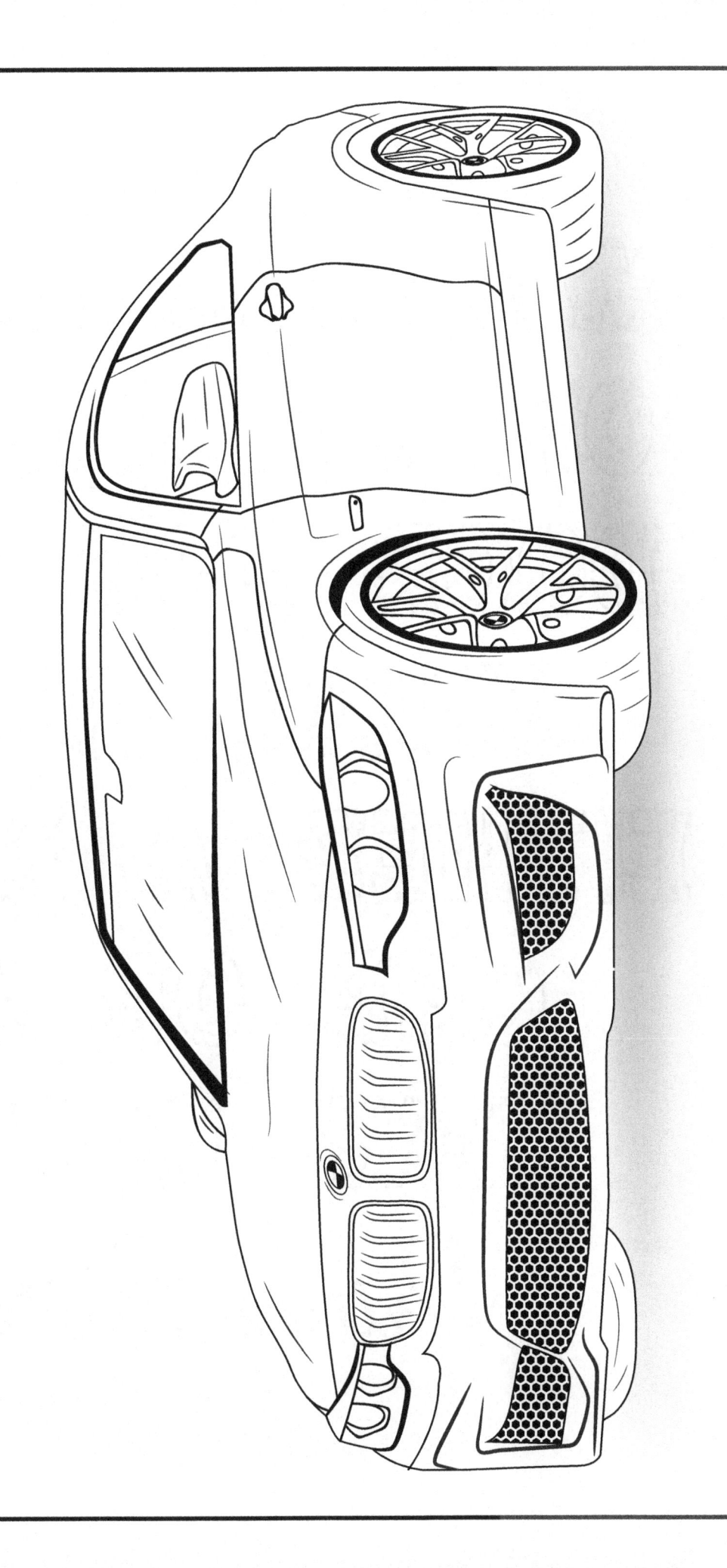

WHEN A MAN OPENS A CAR DOOR FOR HIS WIFE, IT'S EITHER A NEW CAR OR A NEW WIFE.

Prince Philip

ASTON MARTIN DB 11

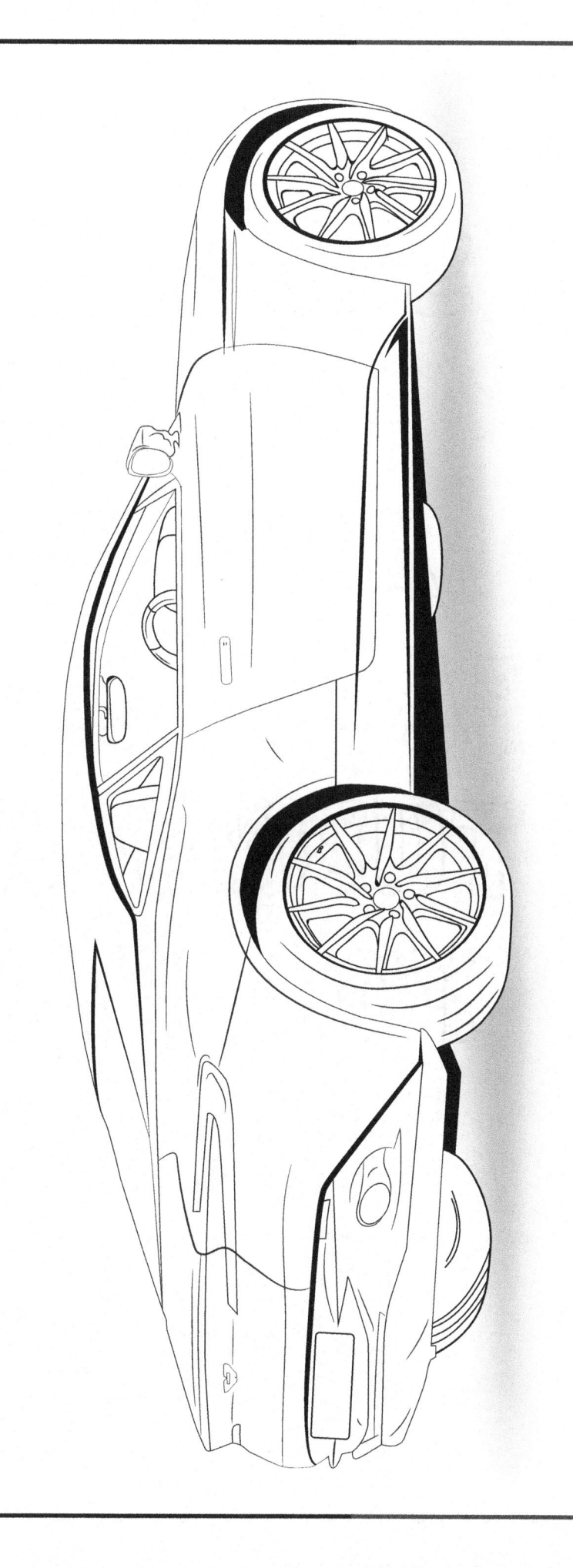

"STRAIGHT ROADS ARE FOR FAST CARS, TURNS ARE FOR FAST DRIVERS."

Colin McRae

FERRARI ROMA

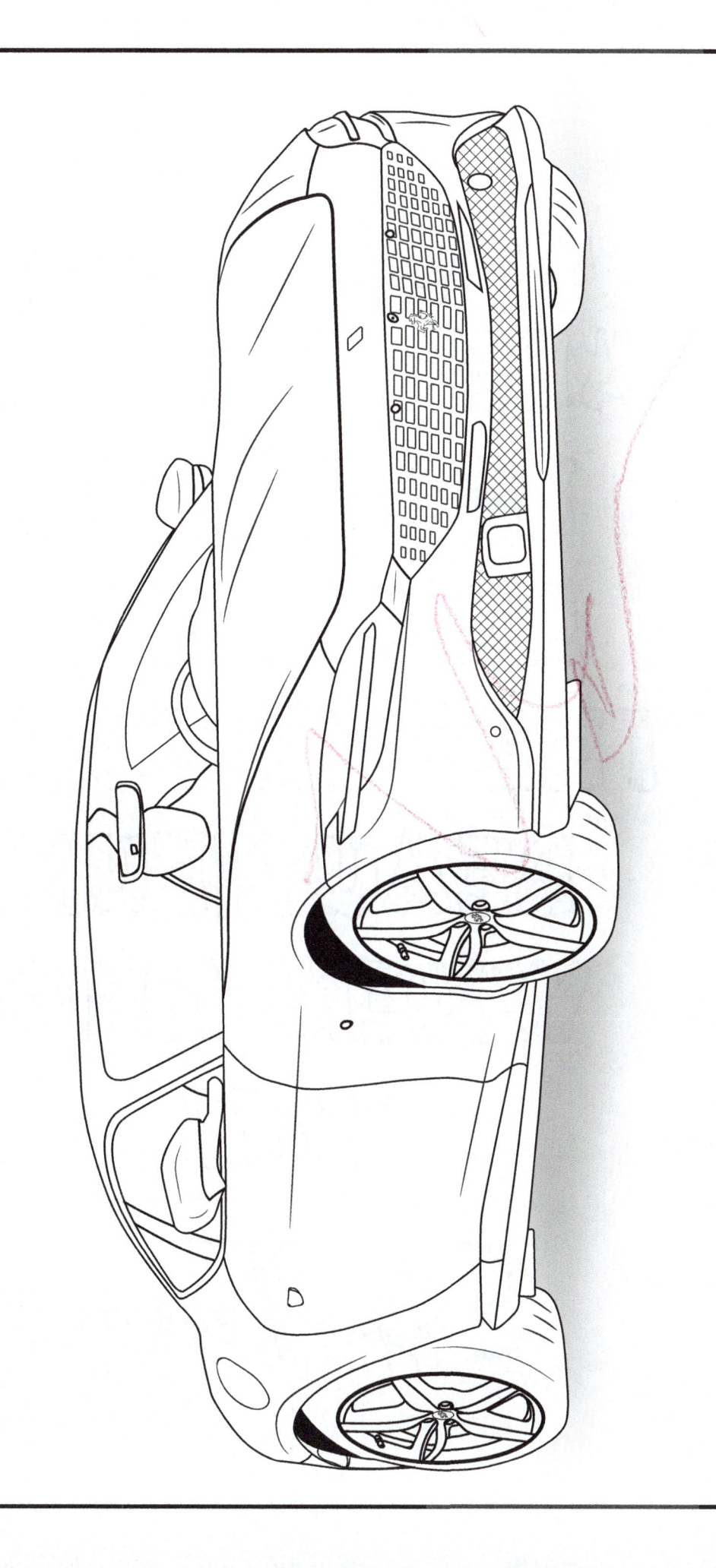

RACE CARS ARE NEITHER BEAUTIFUL NOR UGLY. THEY BECOME BEAUTIFUL WHEN THEY WIN.

Enzo Ferrari

MCLAREN 600 LT

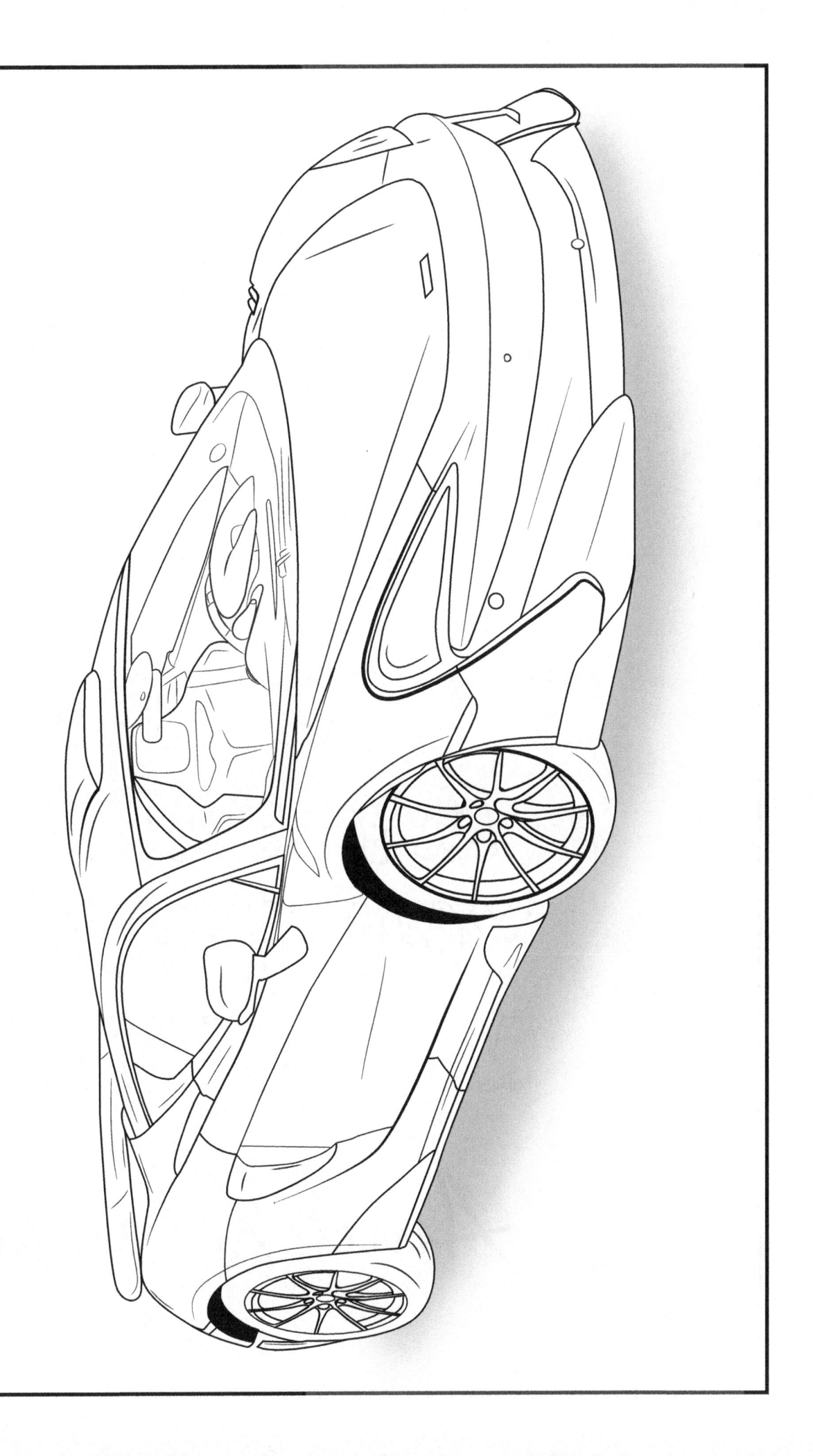

I AM EMOTIONAL ABOUT ENGINES, IF YOU HURT MY CAR, YOU HURT MY HEART.

Amit Kalantri

MERCEDES-BENZ SL 63 AMG

Have you ever noticed that anybody driving slower than you is an idiot, and anyone going faster than you is a maniac?

George Carlin

SUBARU STi PERFORMANCE CONCEPT

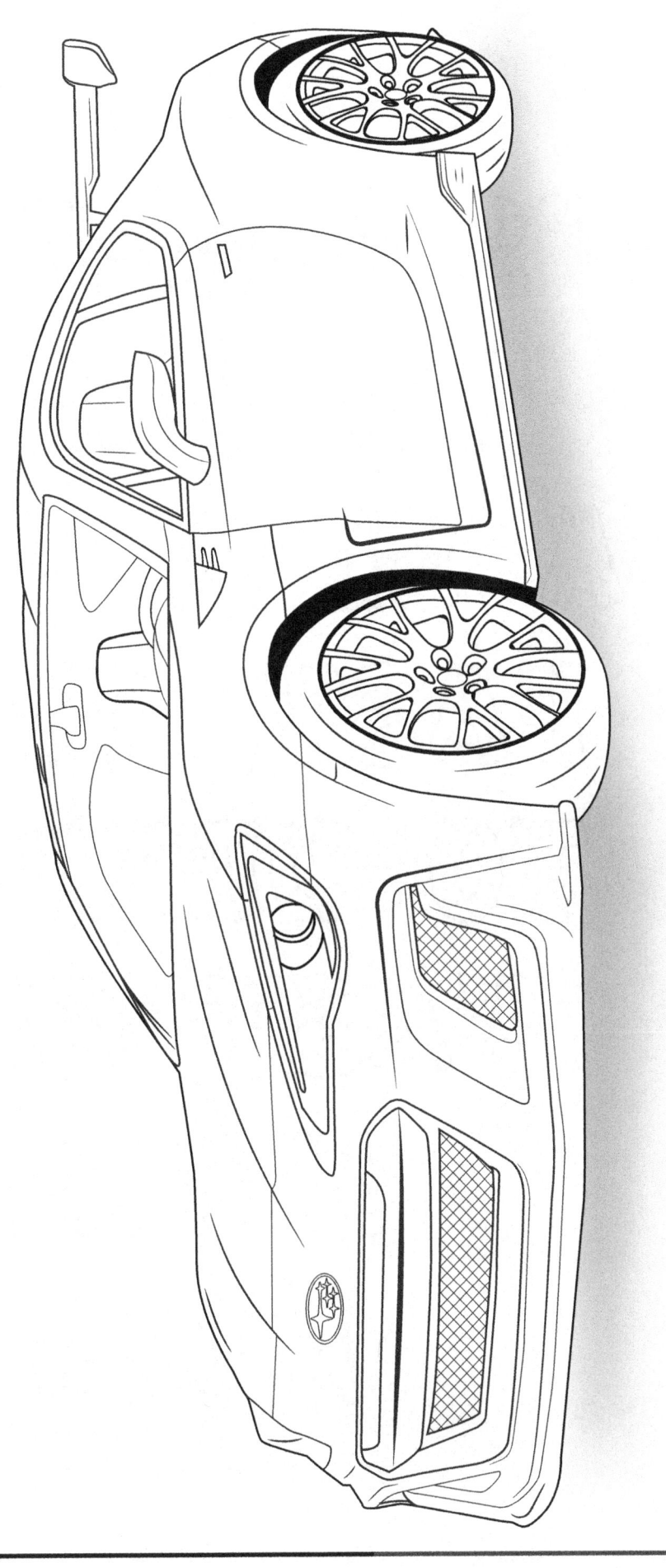

It's more fun to drive a slow car fast, then to drive a fast car slow.

Unknown

TOYOTA SUPRA

IF YOU'RE IN CONTROL, YOU'RE NOT GOING FAST ENOUGH.

Parnelli Jones

BENTLEY CONTINENTAL

All of those cars were once just a dream in somebody's head.

Peter Gabriel

BMW M8 COMPETITION

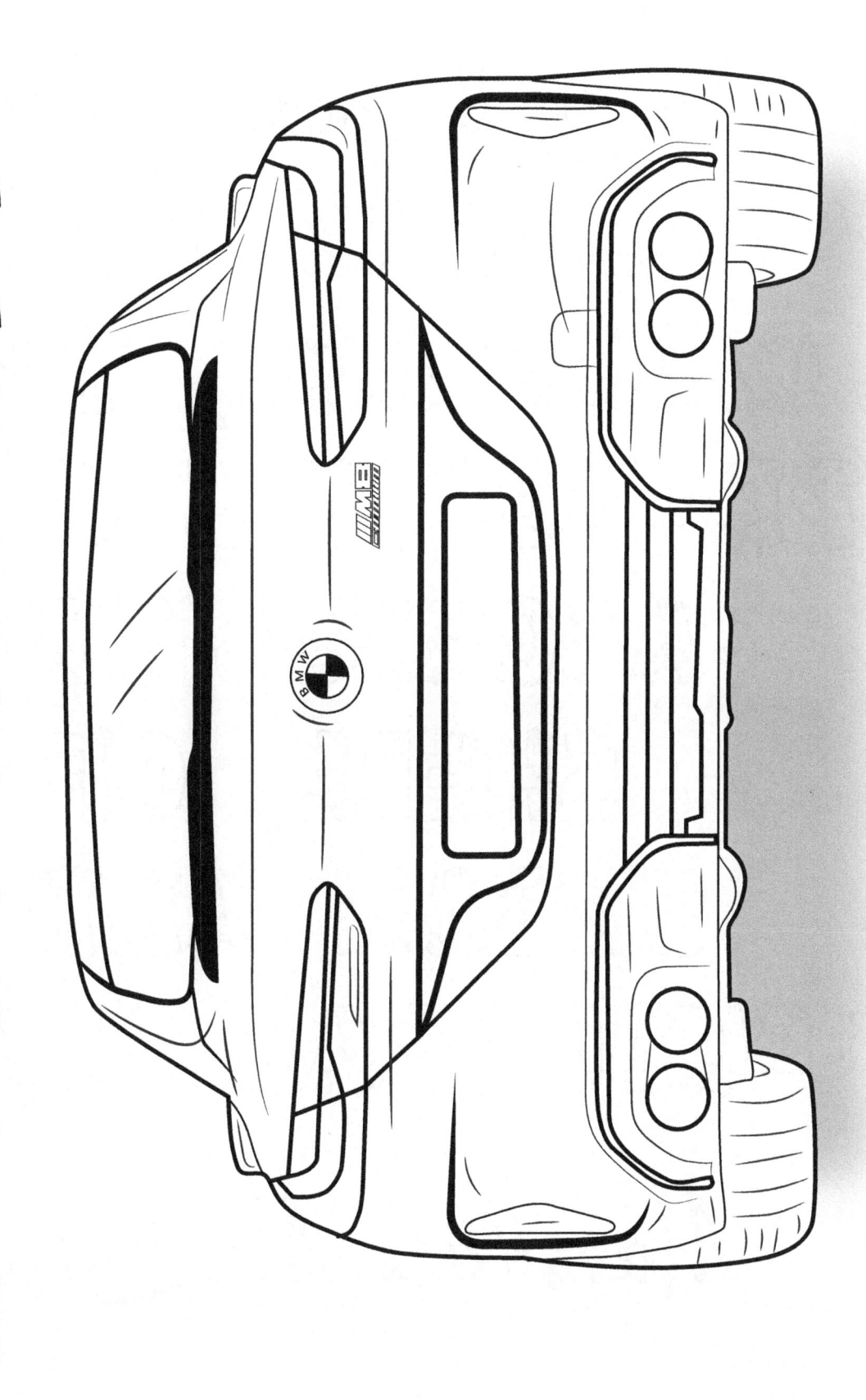

The car has become the carapace, the protective and aggressive shell, of urban and suburban man.

Marshall McLuhan

BUGATTI LA VOITURE NOIRE

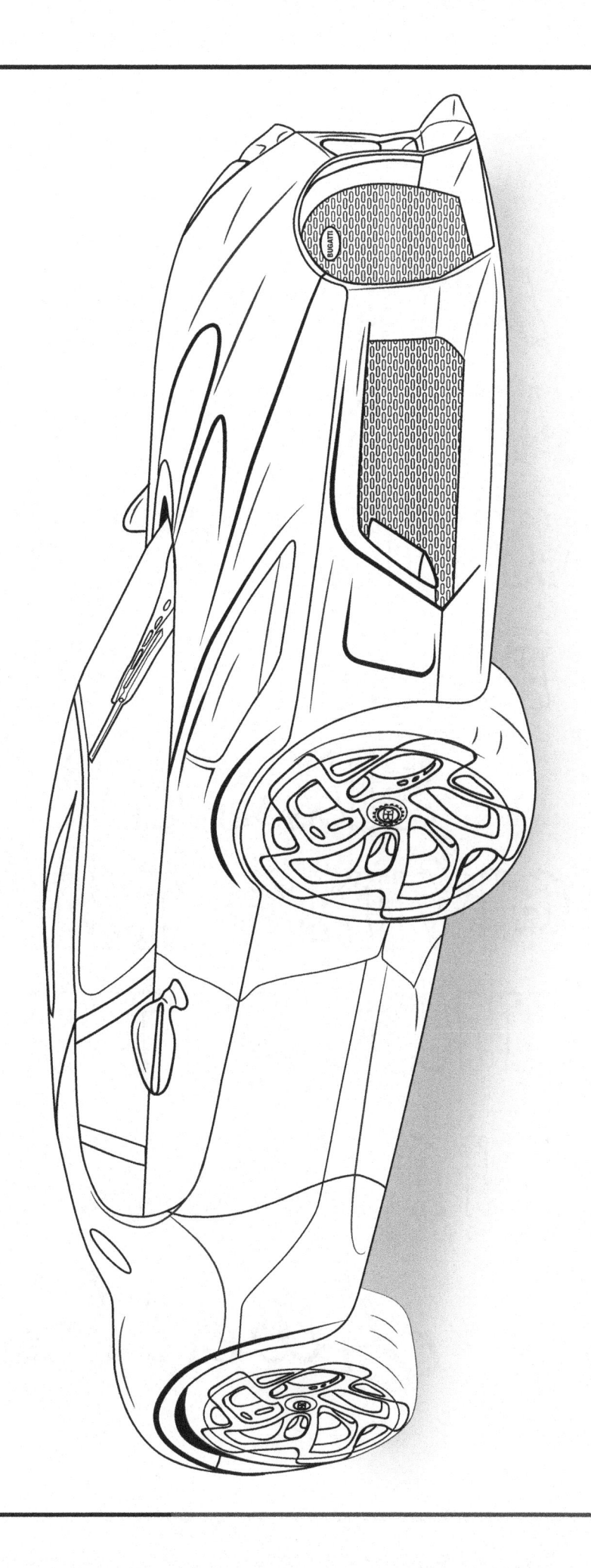

Any man who can drive safely while kissing a pretty girl is simply not giving the kiss the attention it deserves.

Albert Einstein

HONDA CIVIC TYPE R

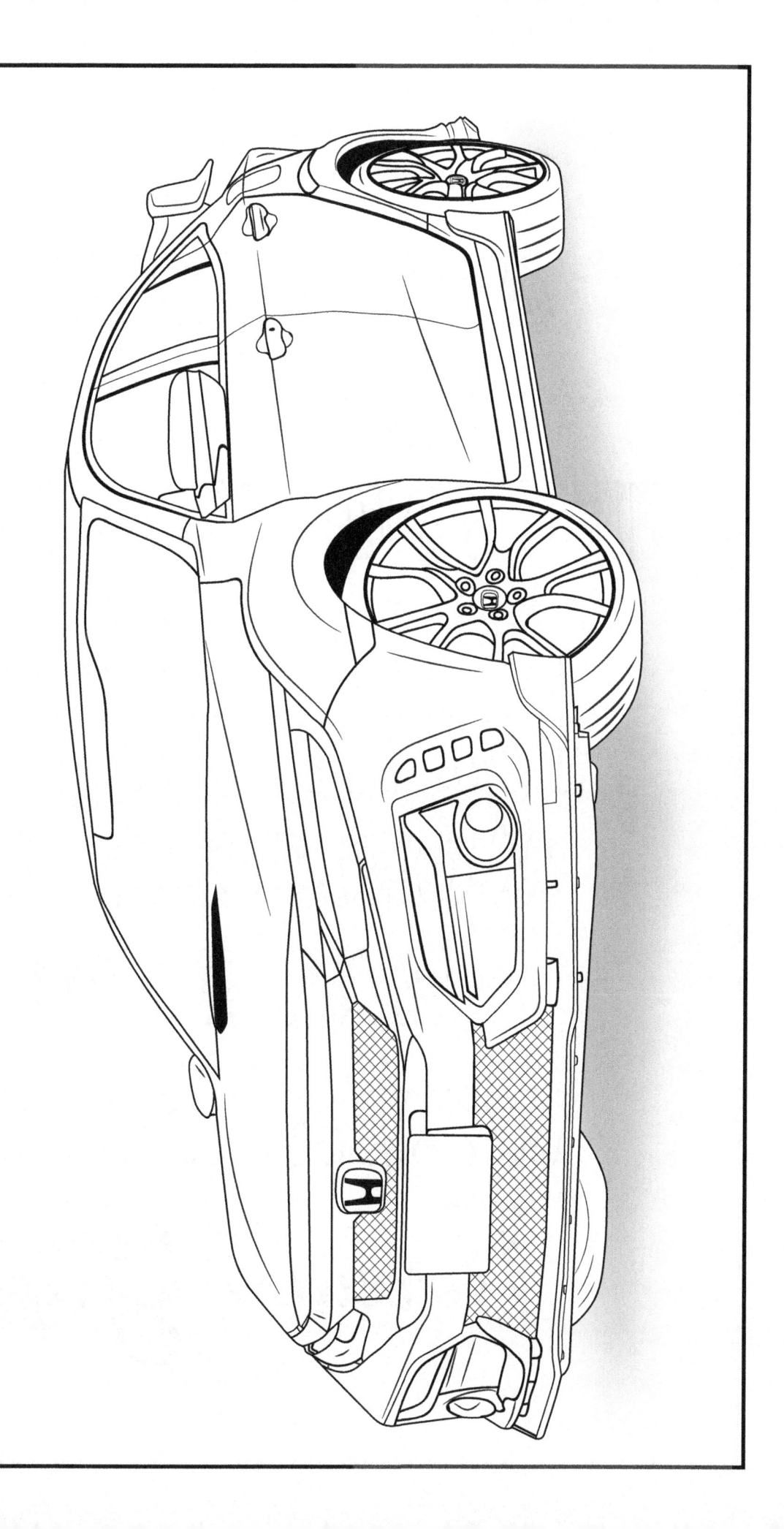

A MUSCLE IS LIKE A CAR. IF YOU WANT IT TO RUN WELL EARLY IN THE MORNING, YOU HAVE TO WARM IT UP.

Florence Griffith

LAMBORGHINI HURACAN STO

CARS ARE THE SCULPTURES OF OUR EVERYDAY LIVES.

Chris Bangle

LAMBORGHINI MIURA P400

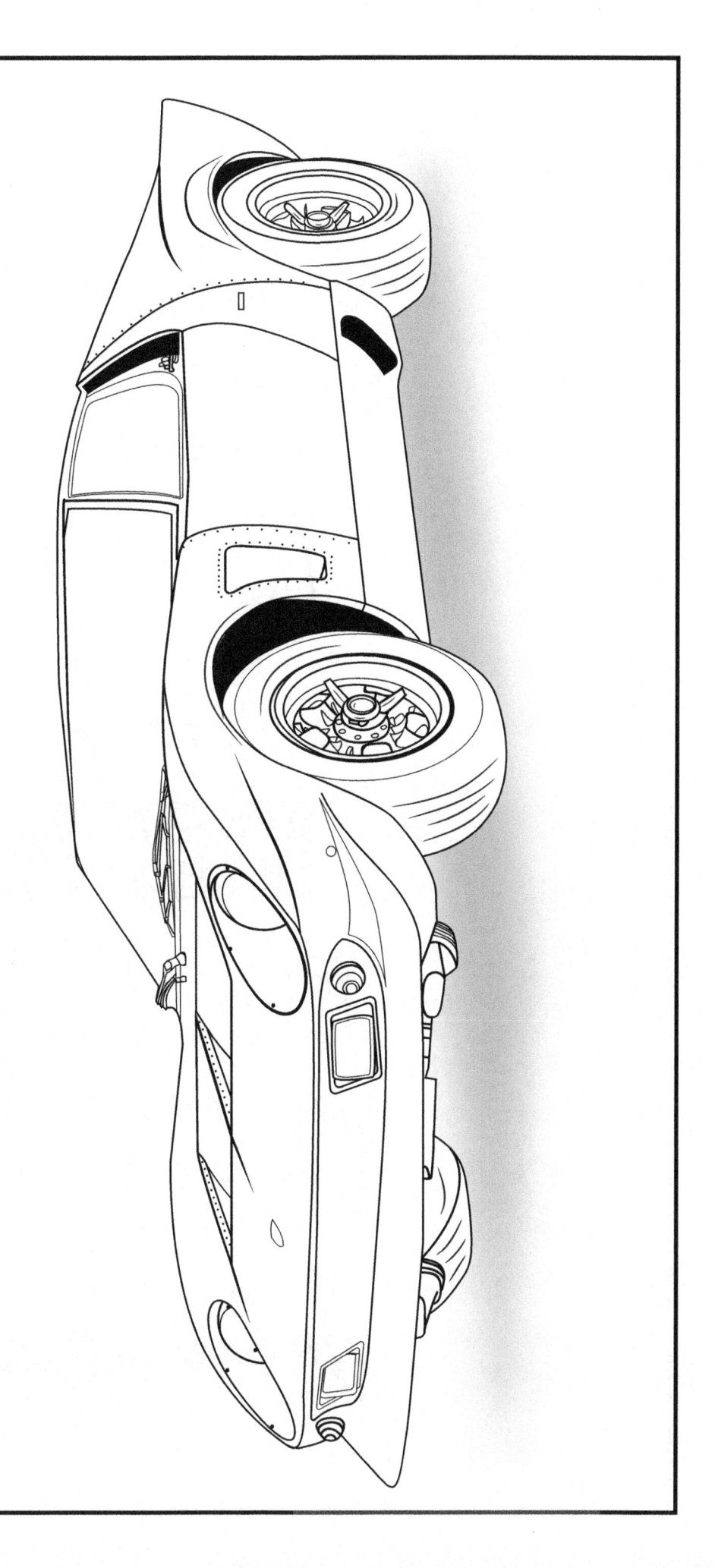

CAR IS SIMPLY NEAR AND DEAR TO MY HEART..

John Lasseter

RANGE ROVER EVOQUE

Some men take good care of a car; others treat it like one of the family.

Evan Esar

ROLLS-ROYCE WRAITH

I think about cars to try and distract myself. It's a good way to relax, take your mind off everything.

Asafa Powell

CHARGE ELECTRIC FORD MUSTANG

A CAR FOR EVERY PURSE AND PURPOSE.

Alfred P. Sloan

BENTLEY CONTINENTAL

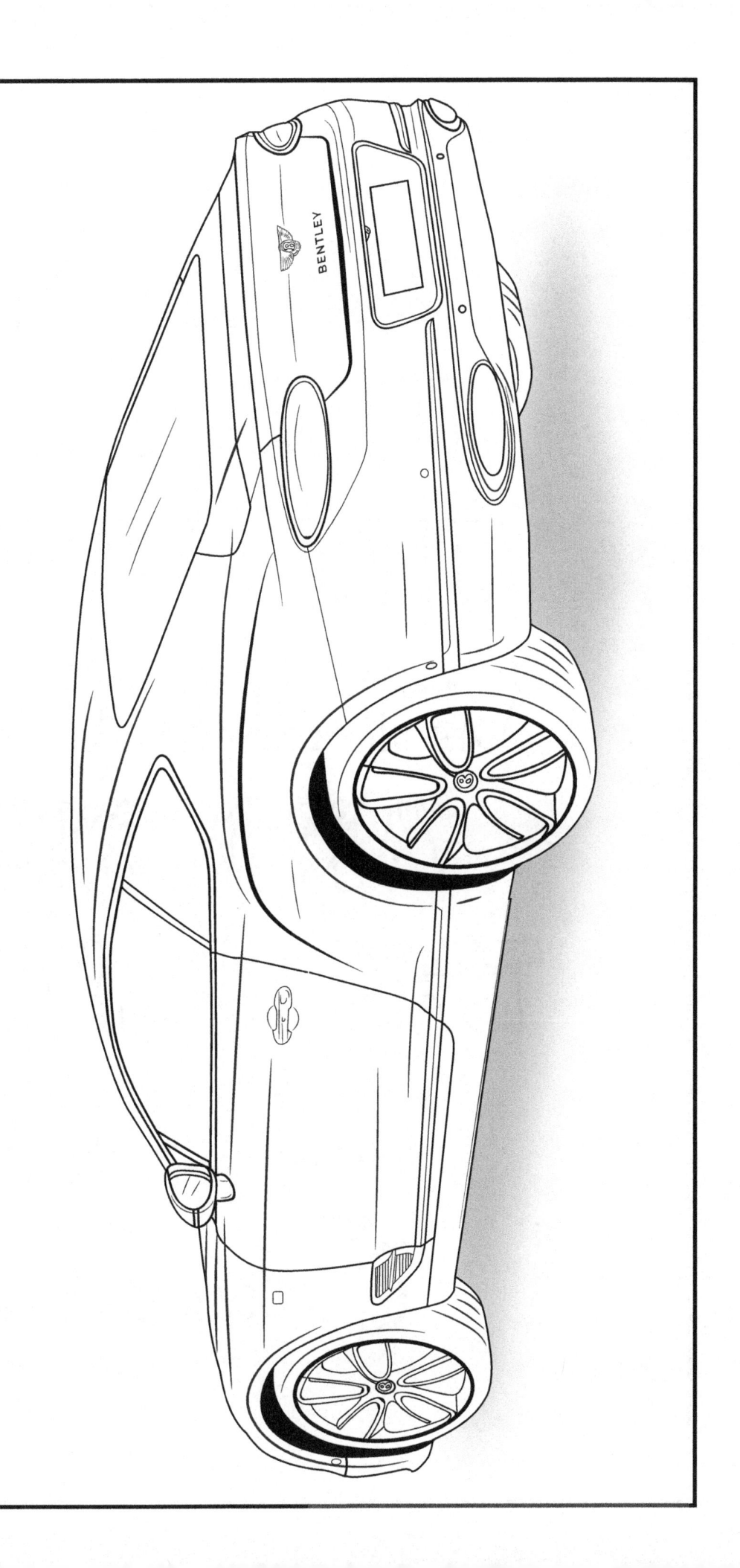

ALWAYS FOCUS ON THE FRONT WINDSHIELD AND NOT THE REVIEW MIRROR.

Colin Powell

ALFA ROMEO GIULIA QUADRIFOGLIO

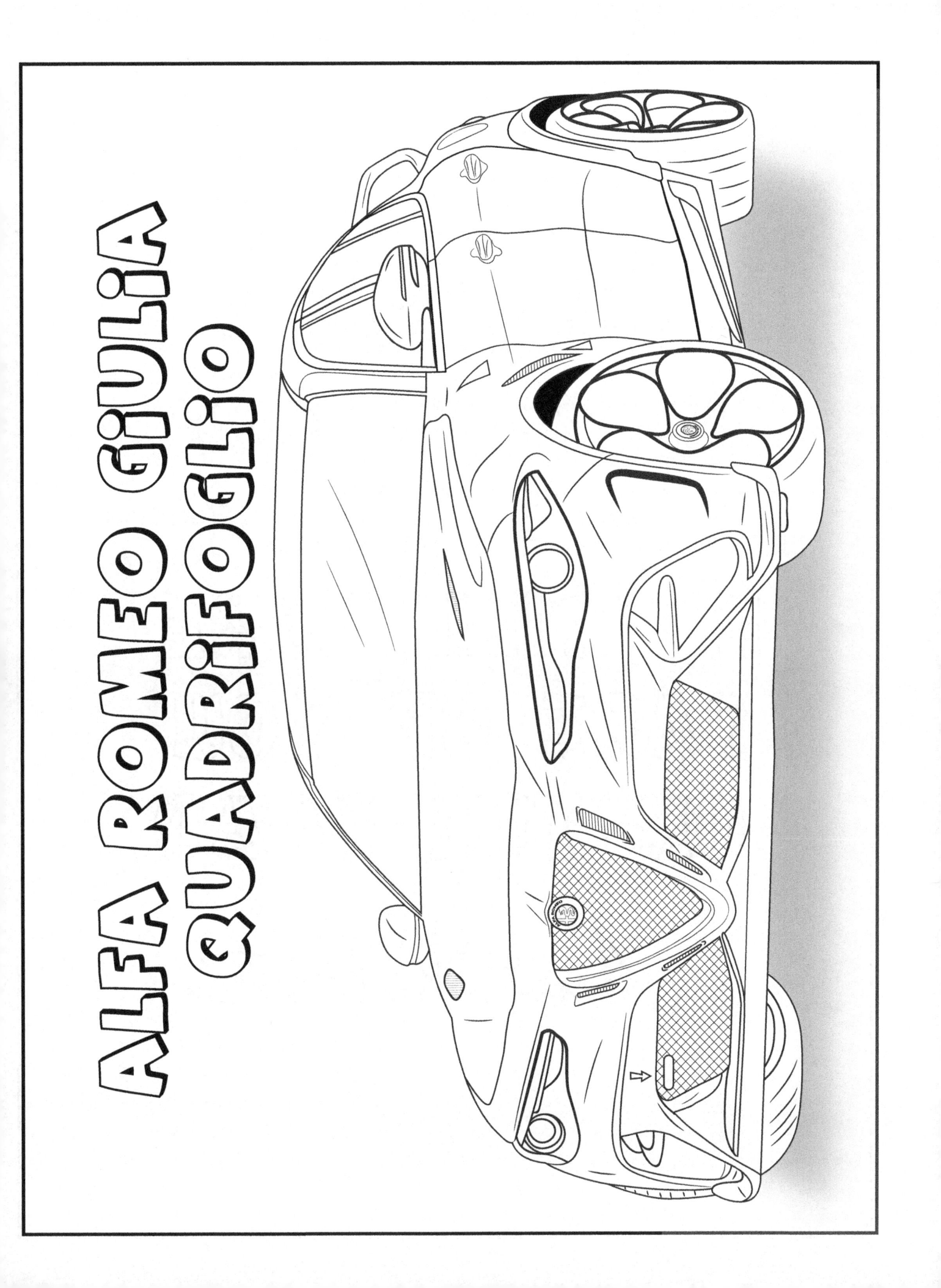

"Take care of your car in the garage; it will take care of you on the road."

— Amit Kalantri

BMW i8

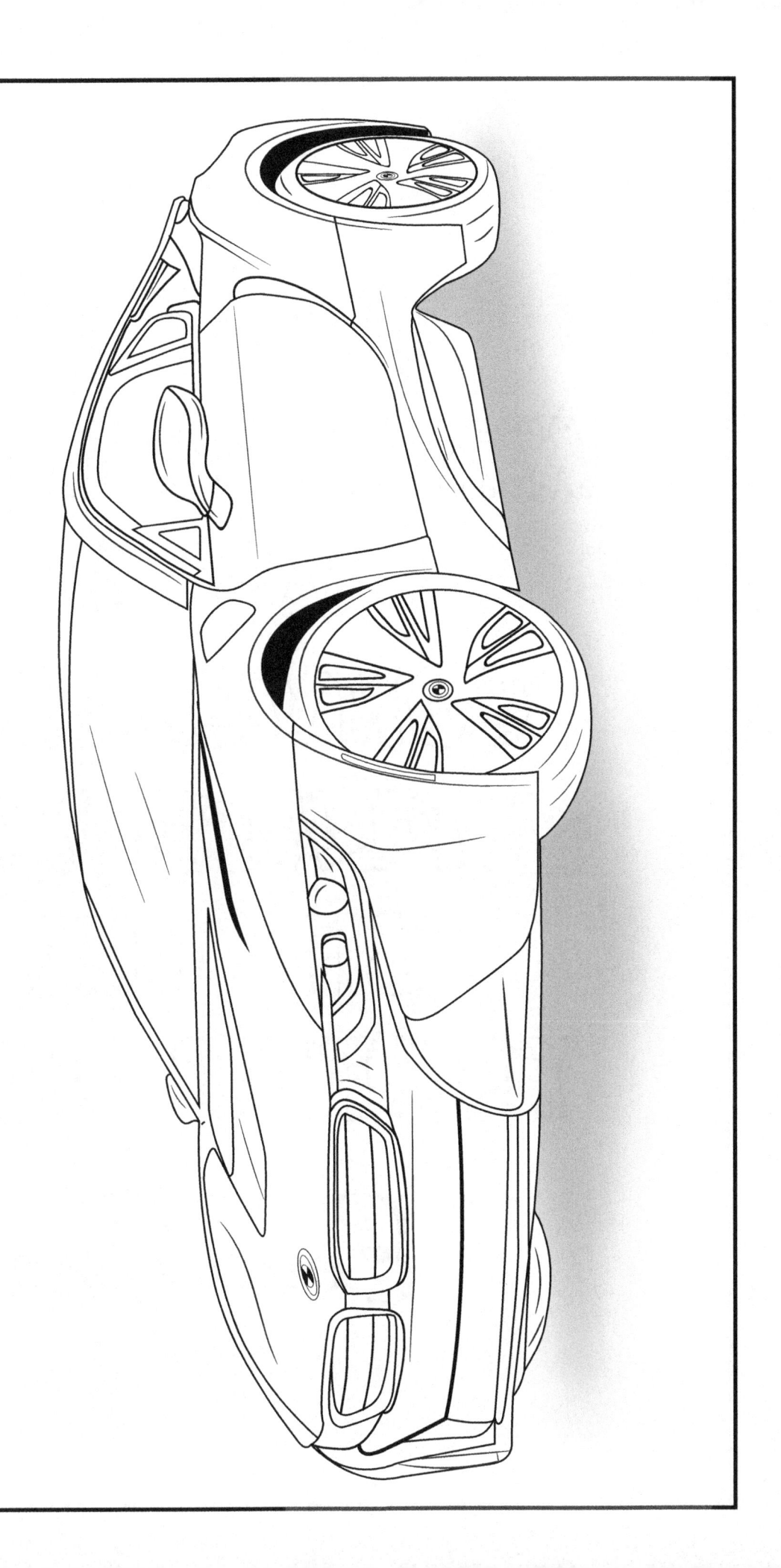

THE CAR
WAS INVENTED
AS A
CONVENIENT
PLACE TO
SIT OUT
TRAFFIC JAMS.

Evan Esar

CHEVROLET CORVETTE C7

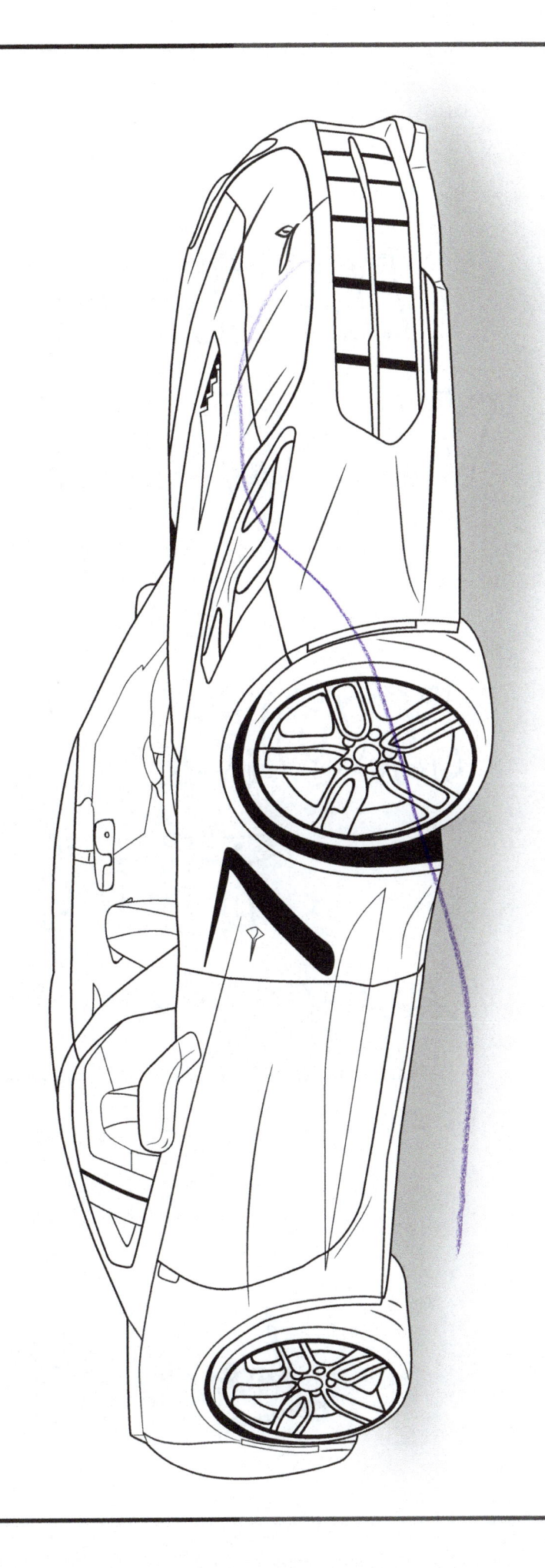

MEN LOVE WOMEN, BUT EVEN MORE THAN THAT, THEY LOVE CARS

Lord Hesketh

LOTUS EXIGE SPORT 410

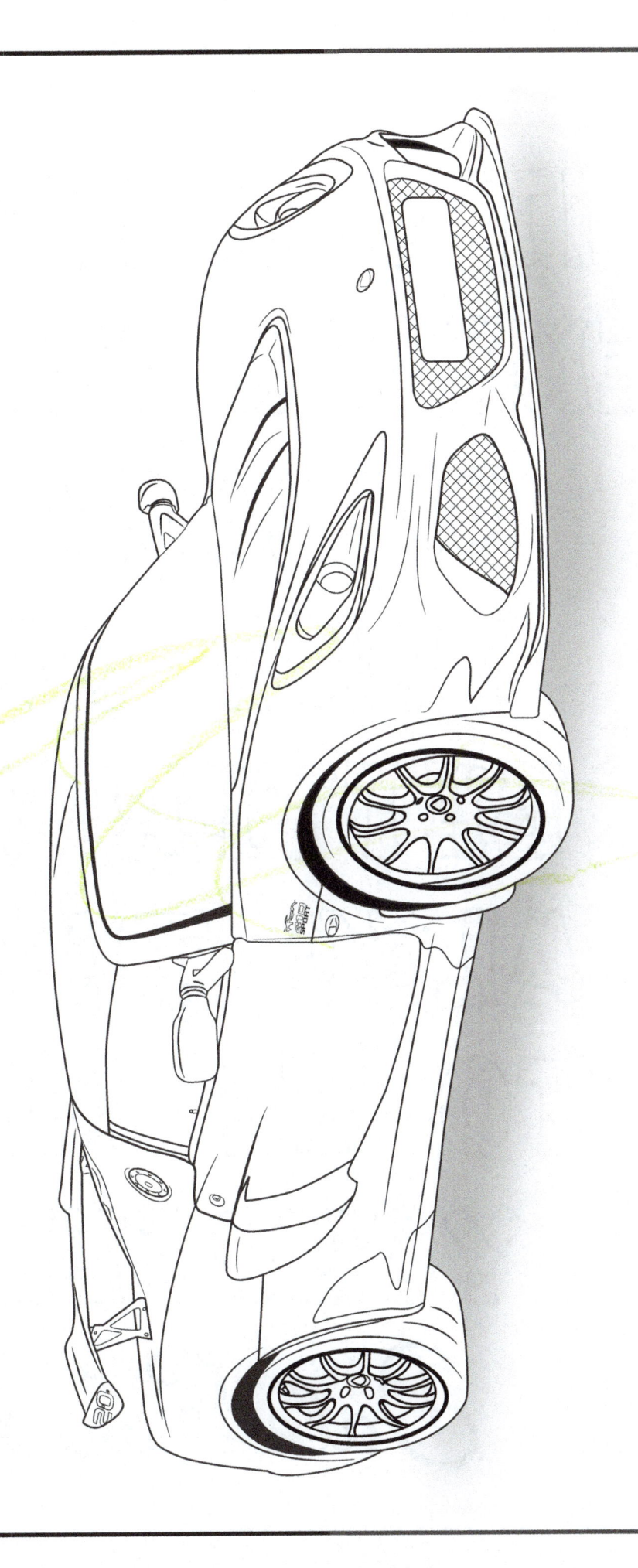

"It's a never-ending battle of making your cars better and also trying to be better yourself."
— Dale Earnhardt

MCLAREN 720S

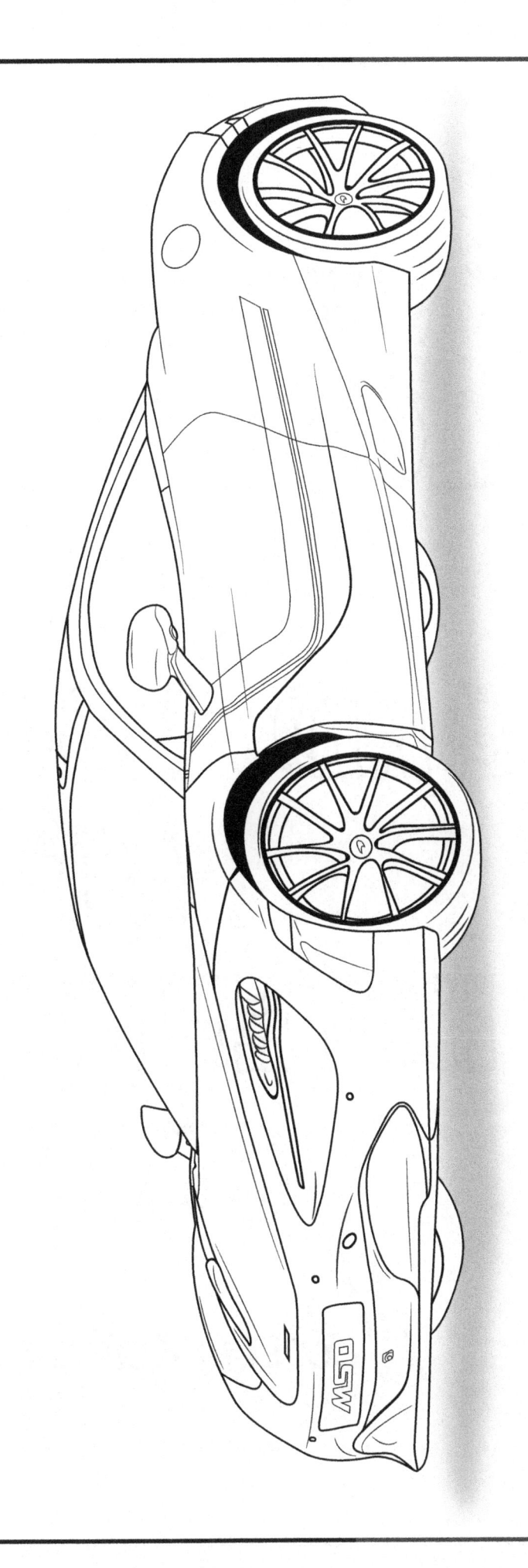

I'VE ALWAYS LOVED FAST VEHICLES AND LOOKING AT INTERESTING CARS.

Ndamukong Suh

PORSCHE 991 TURBO S

WHEN YOU ARE FITTED IN A RACING CAR AND YOU RACE TO WIN SECOND OR THIRD PLACE IS NOT ENOUGH.

Ayrton Senna

ASTON MARTIN
VANQUISH

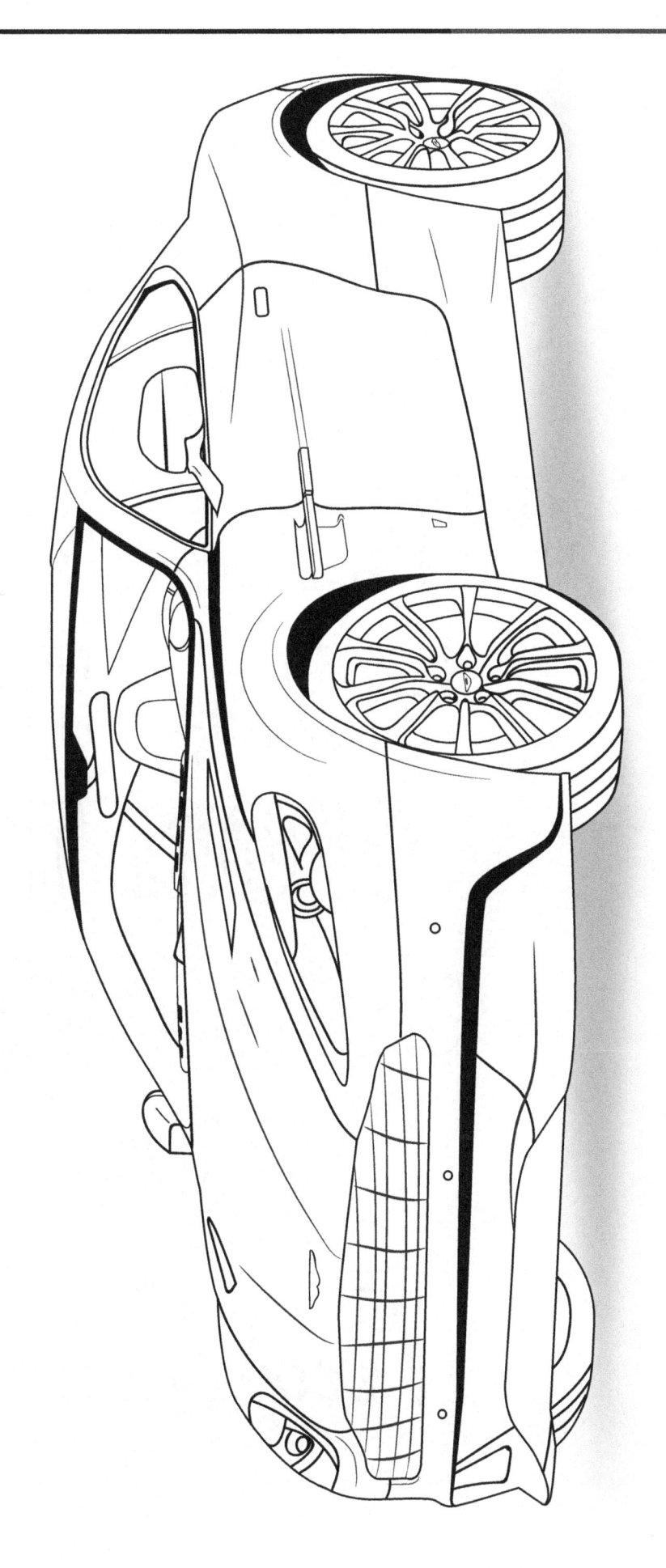

IF IT DOESN'T CHALLENGE YOU, IT WON'T CHANGE YOU.

Fred Devito

ROLLS-ROYCE
CULLINAN

I love driving cars, looking at them, cleaning and washing and shining them. I clean 'em inside and outside. I'm very touchy about cars. I don't want anybody leaning on them or closing the door too hard, know what I mean?

Scott Baio

ASTON MARTIN VANTAGE

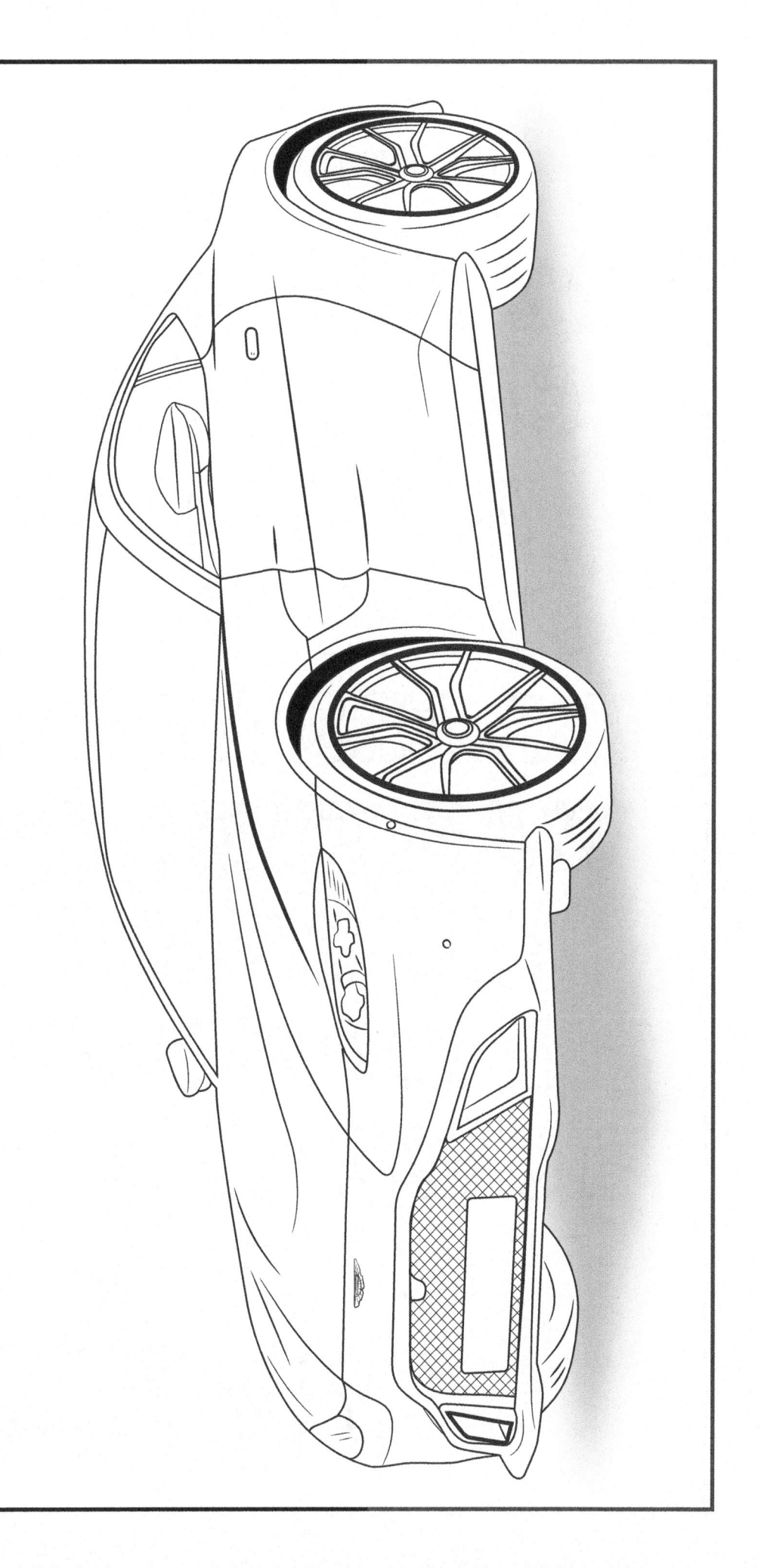

I HATE WHEN SOMEONE DRIVES MY CAR AND RESETS ALL THE RADIO PRESETS. I DON'T UNDERSTANDIT. IF I WAS EVER DRIVING SOMEONE'S CAR, I WOULD NEVER TOUCH THE THINGS THAT WERE SET.

Will Ferrell

Made in the USA
Coppell, TX
25 March 2022